D1438629

Praise for the Book

'This is a thriller-like account of two battles at Nathu La and Cho La between India and China in 1967 that did not get the pride of place in military history and public memory that they deserved. They occurred at a particularly difficult time for India.

'This engagingly written page-turner of a book tells the forgotten story of the 1967 battles of Nathu La and Cho La and brave soldiers like Sagat Singh, Bishan Singh and P. S. Dagar who banished the ghosts of the 1962 defeat and of diplomats and spies engaging in a tit-for-tat intrigue.

'India didn't gain new territory in 1967 and lost 100 lives. But it gained something far more important – its self-esteem and an era of peace. This is a valuable addition to the still thin genre of military historiography in India.'

Shekhar Gupta, chairman and editor-in-chief, *Print*

'*Watershed 1967* is an exhilarating narrative of a set of high-altitude battles at Nathu La and Cho La in September 1967 that marked the revival of India's military confidence in its dealings with China. Meticulously researched amidst the backdrop of the 1965 India–Pakistan conflict and rising tensions between India and China over the status of Sikkim. Probal DasGupta is a gifted storyteller with a real feel for battle.'

**Air Vice Marshal Arjun Subramaniam (retd),
author of *India's Wars: A Military History, 1947–1971***

'Major DasGupta sheds valuable light on some of the lesser-known military interactions between India and China – his focus being the 1967 battles of Cho La and Nathu La where the tricolor prevailed. Written with distinctive verve this book braids battle narratives with international politics, intrigue and insightful authorial reflections. A must-read for the specialist and the lay person alike.'

Commodore C. Uday Bhaskar (retd), director,
Society for Policy Studies

'India vis-a-vis China must not be seen through the prism of the 1962 war as a sore reminder. The bravery of Cho La and Nathu La of 1967, provided the impetus and strength for recent eye-ball confrontations at DBO, Demchock, Chumar and Doklam. Probal DasGupta's *Watershed 1967* is that breath of fresh air which recounts Indian victories, boosts self-esteem and confidence, and lays a new narrative for the 21st century. A welcome addition to the discourse.'

Lieutenant General Rakesh Sharma (retd),
former adjutant general, Indian army

'A book that should forever emblazon 1967's victory against China in India's public consciousness as much as 1962's defeat. A wonderful account of an operation that has never received its due, filled with delectable granularity, both in the political offices and the battlefield.'

Shiv Aroor, co-author of *India's Most Fearless: True Stories of*
Modern Military Heroes

'Sheds light on little-known facts . . . Vignettes of intrigue playing out like moves on a chessboard . . . make Probal DasGupta's book critical for anyone following the India–China competition.'

Husain Haqqani, former Pakistan ambassador to the US and
author of *India vs Pakistan: Why Can't We Just Be Friends?*

Watershed 1967

Watershed 1967

India's Forgotten Victory
Over China

Probal DasGupta

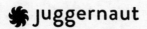

JUGGERNAUT BOOKS
C-I-128, First Floor, Sangam Vihar, Near Holi Chowk,
New Delhi 110080, India

First published by Juggernaut Books 2020

10 9 8 7 6 5 4 3 2

P-ISBN: 9789353450939
E-ISBN: 9789353450946

Typeset in Adobe Caslon Pro by R. Ajith Kumar, Noida

Printed at Thomson Press India Ltd

For Baba,
who will inspire me forever

Contents

Contents

Introduction

India and China are neighbours with much in common. Big land masses, crowded cities, large populations. Between the two countries lives one-third of the human population on earth, histories of many hundreds of years of invasions, brutal oppressions and famines and, of course, Buddhism and the Dalai Lama. They share crucial differences too: ideological distinctions being one (one is a communist dictatorship and another a democracy) and the choice of friends being the other (Pakistan is an all-weather friend to one and foe to the other). Much of their history of the last sixty years though centres around the bitter war the two countries fought in the Himalayas.

The 1962 war, which China won, is a significant event in the relationship and a sore memory for Indians. The dismal defeat dealt a cruel blow to the pride of a grand old civilization and a newly independent country born fifteen years earlier. The impact of that defeat still lingers in Indian thinking about the dangers of antagonizing China.

But unremembered by most people is an equally significant event that took place five years after the 1962 war. India and China fought again in 1967, on two Himalayan passes called Cho La and Nathu La at the China–Sikkim border. This book traces the story of that incredible but forgotten victory over China.

The narrative in this book has been divided into three parts. The story begins in Part 1 three years after the India–China war of 1962. India was still recovering from the damaged morale of its political and military leadership. After the defeat of 1962, India began to acquire weapons and equipment, besides raising multiple army divisions to strengthen its defences. Such rapid developments caught the attention of Pakistani leaders who believed that a better armed and prepared India would be difficult to overwhelm in the future. An alliance against India was entered into between Pakistan and China which suited both countries. For Pakistan, the unresolved issue of Kashmir was a motivation to corner India when it was down, while for China a natural ally such as Pakistan, given the historic India–Pakistan animosity, could be used to fight a convenient proxy war to further establish its dominance over India. In 1965, two vulnerable points – Kashmir in the north and Sikkim in the east – presented an opportunity for China and Pakistan to stretch India's military deployment on both flanks and demolish its defence capabilities. On both fronts there existed narrow geographical corridors whose capture could end up dismembering India.

The book begins with a story of international intrigue and the resultant devious plan hatched by Pakistan and China to attack India in 1965. This well-crafted plan was shrewdly shared with a prominent Kashmiri politician to try to acquire local support for a Pakistani attack against India. Around the same time, American spies and the CIA, aware about the turn of events, were gazing at a potential war involving the three countries – India, China and Pakistan.

War finally broke out between India and Pakistan in August 1965. Pakistan used a combination of covert and conventional approaches to wage war in Kashmir and then in Punjab, while China threatened India's protectorate state of Sikkim, then under the control of monarchy. The plan was to capture Kashmir and occupy Sikkim and then force India to the negotiating table for a barter exchange involving the two states. But India's successful performance in the 1965 war against Pakistan foiled the Sino-Pakistani plans. China's threat on the eastern border, though, remained unresolved. The war ended with India acquiring an edge over Pakistan but also resulted in a permanent Chinese presence on the Sikkim border. The stage was set for India and China to face off in Sikkim.

The second part of the book traces the events from the end of the 1965 war and leads into the historic battles of 1967. Sikkim's royals wanted Sikkim to be an independent state, much to the annoyance of the government in New Delhi. And China tried constantly to bully and browbeat India. There were frequent disputes between New Delhi and Peking (now Beijing) in this period on issues such as Bhutan's territory of Doklam and China's support to insurgency movements in India, including the new Naxal movement inside Bengal. These were years when things were constantly on the boil: there were frequent skirmishes on the Sikkim–China border, and even the arrest of two Indian diplomats in Peking and the tit-for-tat mistreatment of Chinese diplomats in New Delhi. Atal Bihari Vajpayee even led a flock of sheep to the gates of the Chinese embassy in Delhi to protest Peking's belligerence.

Relations were on a slippery slope. The armies of the two countries clashed in Nathu La in September 1967 over the laying of a barbed wire fence to mark the Sikkim–China border. The battle lasted a few days. Under the leadership of Lieutenant General Sagat Singh, young officers and soldiers of the Indian army defeated the Chinese at Nathu La. Many lives were lost on both sides but the Indians finally got their revenge against the Chinese for the humiliation of 1962. Embarrassed and shell-shocked, the Chinese engaged the Indians again fifteen days later in another battle at Cho La, in the same sector. Once again, Sagat's forces proved more than equal to the task. The Chinese were defeated again and this time, the psychological burden of being beaten in two successive battles within a month befell China.

The third part of the book explores the strategic aftermath of the victories at Nathu La and Cho La. The victories of 1967 and Sagat Singh's audacious decision at that time to occupy the border at Nathu La, ignoring the Chinese threat and even defying the orders of his superiors, played a decisive role in China not participating actively in the India–Pakistan war of 1971. The vulnerability of the Siliguri Corridor, the thin strip of land that links the north-eastern part of India to the rest of its land, and which China would have had easy access to had it won the battle of Nathu La, could not have been felt more than during the 1971 war. Had China had control over Nathu La it could have linked up with East Pakistani forces easily and severed India's eastern wing from the mainland. But the victories in the battles of 1967 prevented Chinese interference in the Siliguri Corridor in 1971 – something that saved India from certain disaster.

India's watershed victories are unrecognized turning points in history and helped shape India's approach to later conflicts with China. These battles determined the military template for India's aggressive performance in stand-offs such as in Sumdorong Chu in 1986 and Doklam in 2017. Fifty years after these battles, China and India have never fought a war again. There are many important reasons for this but the role of the 1967 battles in creating a template to grapple with military confrontation cannot be underestimated.

The twin victories at Cho La and Nathu La have only been covered in fragments through articles and papers. This book, based on extensive interviews with the army men who were present at the scene, captures the events truthfully and aims to fix this blind spot in history. This was personally important to me, being a former army officer myself.

Today, Nathu La is a bustling tourist attraction on the India–China border. Thousands of visitors flock the border where Indian and Chinese sentries stand opposite each other. The tales of the soldiers' sacrifices at these Himalayan heights to restore a nation's self-esteem and usher in an era of peace is unparalleled. It is the story of India's forgotten victory over China – the last time they fought.

Part 1

The Road to 1967

1

Secret Games: Spies, Soldiers and the Opening Gambit

It is the first day of October in the year 1967. Debi Prasad and his fellow Indian soldiers are engaged in a fierce battle with the Chinese at the Cho La pass on the Sikkim–China border. Letting out the war cry 'Jai Maa Kali, Ayo Gorkhali', the young Gorkha turns into a raging tiger, and rushes towards the well-armed Chinese soldiers. In a flash, he draws out the deadly khukri from the scabbard, raises it to the sky and brings it down on the Chinese light machine gunner before his forefinger can pull the trigger.

Debi moves like lightning as he swipes, swings and slashes, letting the traditional shiny dagger heave and strike in a fearsome display of hand-to-hand combat. He scythes through the Chinese forward line of defence, lopping off five heads as

9

soldiers fall around him. The collective might of the enemy front line is not enough to stop this short, sturdy young man. By the time a desperate bullet knocks him dead, Debi Prasad has destroyed the much-vaunted Chinese defensive wall.

Debi's khukri continues to haunt the Chinese. His heroics steered India towards certain victory, an outcome that would change Indo-China relations forever.

However, the seeds of India's battles with China in 1967 had been sown two years earlier, in 1965, when signs of a sinister design had begun to show, far, far away.

~

Jeddah, the ancient port city in Saudi Arabia, off the Red Sea, is a window to the trading world and a staging post for pilgrims. Since the seventh century CE, it has been a major port for Indian Ocean trade routes. The setting of the *Arabian Nights*, Jeddah is a land of mysteries and secrets.

Sometime in early 1965, Duane Ramsdell Clarridge flew into Jeddah from Washington, DC to meet a man who had promised him a dangerous secret.[1] Duane knew it could be a wild goose chase. He was no stranger to disappointments. Yet there he was on this unpredictable trail.

While waiting for his source in the old city, Duane hoped it would be worth the long flight. After all, it was the culmination of a pursuit that had begun a few years ago when he lived in India. When the source finally appeared and revealed the secret, Duane was left quaking in his boots. Little did he know that this would become a decisive point in history.

Born to a dentist father, Duane grew up in a staunch republican family[2] in Nashua, New Hampshire. A neighbour nicknamed him Dewey, after Thomas E. Dewey, the New York governor who ran for president against Franklin D. Roosevelt in 1944.[3] Handsome and articulate, he attended Brown University and then the Columbia School of International and Public Affairs before joining the CIA in 1955[4] hoping for a chance to fight communists. Instead, he found himself posted in India where much of his time was spent socializing, playing polo in Delhi and cultivating new informants in Madras.[5]

Having developed a bulldog tenacity and sharp instincts when it came to gathering intelligence, Dewey had his eye on Sheikh Abdullah, a charismatic but controversial politician. The government in New Delhi, headed by Jawaharlal Nehru, viewed him as a political dissident, a Kashmiri rebel. Abdullah had become the prime minister of Jammu and Kashmir (J&K) in 1948.

In 1953 he was deposed and imprisoned without charges being brought against him. He was released briefly in 1958 but arrested again, this time on charges of being a Pakistani agent. When finally released on 8 April 1964, he was greeted by a throng of twenty-odd-thousand people, and that's when he had Dewey's full attention. He was rangy and statuesque with the magnetic appeal of a beloved community leader. He bared an unusually large set of teeth every time he smiled. He was warm and impulsive at the same time, the kind of source the CIA liked to cultivate. Upon his release from prison he left for Paris.[6] That's how, later that year, Dewey found himself walking down a dingy lane on the left bank in Paris which brought him to the nondescript hotel where Abdullah was staying.

'I am from the US government. I'd like to come and speak with you,' he said into the house phone at the reception by way of an introduction.[7] Soon, a nervous and tentative Dewey was rushing up the rickety hotel stairs to finally come face to face with Abdullah. Unfortunately, the meeting turned out to be a damp squib and ended with Abdullah promising to meet again with crucial information, this time in Jeddah.

Dewey was certain this wasn't a fruitless pursuit, for he had sensed Abdullah was no ordinary fellow – he was likely in on a huge international secret.

Abdullah had been touring several countries after his release and his remarks on Kashmir had stirred up a controversy. An article he had written in an American magazine advocating self-determination for Kashmir had attracted in equal measure approval from Pakistan and criticism from India. His actions had put him on the radars of the Chinese and Pakistani authorities. It was in their interest to cultivate a dissident Kashmiri leader with mass support whom India was wary of.

A few months after meeting Dewey in Paris, Abdullah was in Algiers in February 1965 to attend the second Asian African Conference where he met the Chinese premier Zhou Enlai.[8] Zhou, an otherwise discreet politician, revealed a plan that Pakistan and China were hatching in concert. While he was on Haj around the same time that year, Pakistani emissaries approached him and confirmed the news. They sought his response to a potential Pakistani and Chinese stratagem of attacking India. Abdullah's reaction was said to be favourable,[9] which would have assured the Pakistani leadership that military action taken by its army against India in Kashmir would be supported by the local population.

The news Dewey brought back to the CIA headquarters from Jeddah was sensational: Pakistan was going to attack Kashmir in the late summer of 1965.[10] The details he provided were exhaustive: Pakistani guerrilla units would quietly infiltrate Kashmir and instigate a popular uprising. Kashmir would burn and while the Indian authorities were occupied there, regular Pakistani troops would launch a full-blown conventional attack. The aim was to cut off Kashmir from the rest of India. After occupying the state, Pakistan would force India to give up Kashmir. Supporting them militarily in this plan was China.

While the news made Dewey's hair stand on end, the response from Langley was anticlimactic. The young, ambitious spy's excitement was quelled by a seemingly routine, phlegmatic indifference. Sure as he was about his information, he was still relatively new in the headquarters and intimidated by the chain of command.[11] The CIA had suspected that a military arrangement was evolving between China and Pakistan, which could include a plan to attack India. Dewey's information confirmed this and also revealed that a guerilla attack would precede the conventional war, which was news to the CIA.

~

February mornings at the government-supported think tank Institute of Defence Analyses in Arlington, Virginia, were usually slow and relaxed. However, one Thursday morning in February 1965 the institute was unusually busy, with a motley group of scholars, analysts and political scientists milling about. They had gathered to engage in a simulation of potential international conflicts between nations which would either be resolved peacefully or by resorting to war. They called it the crisis game. Previously, the institute had reconstructed past conflicts between adversaries to gauge outcomes of hypothetical situations. For instance, the Cuban missile crisis of 1962 that brought the Americans and the Soviets close to war helped formulate a crucial crisis game at Arlington. That day the issue was a potential conflict in South Asia, focused on three players – India, Pakistan and China. They tested battle scenarios: planned air raids, military offensives and defensive bulwarks, ran logistics trains and pitched diplomatic counters. This time was different because the conflict had yet to take place.

One of the operating tenets of the crisis game was to ensure the situations were hypothetical.[12] However, the scenario set up for the game that day, with its naming of Kashmir as a focal point of the conflict, was strikingly close to ground reality. The game supposed an Indian subcontinent divided and bloodied by recent conflict – which it most certainly was. As Gautam Das notes in *China–Tibet–India: The 1962 War and the Strategic Military Future*, India and Pakistan had battled briefly in 1948 and then India fought China in 1962 – when it met with a disastrous defeat against its northern neighbour. The incident has also been mentioned by Bertil Lintner (*China's India War*) and Neville Maxwell (*India's China War*).

The players of the crisis game noted that this defeat had exposed how ineffectual Indian defence preparedness was. An avowedly non-aligned nation that leaned towards the communist state of USSR, India had been forced to call upon the United States for aid when the Chinese forces threatened a deeper invasion. Pakistan, on the other hand, was seen as a rising economy, an anti-communist state that had been admitted as a member of the Southeast Asia Treaty Organization (SEATO), a regional defence organization of nations formed in 1954 to prevent the influence of the Soviets and communism on the countries in the region. Pakistan was a regular recipient of military aid from the United States.

The participants of the game analysed the growing and bitter rivalry between India and Pakistan and assessed their political and military strengths. The two newly free nations were charting separate paths: Pakistan, the smaller of the two, was a capitalist economy, led by a grizzled military veteran who hated the USSR, loved Americans, liked horses and whisky. He was, according to the Americans, the good guy – though his good standing would not last much longer. India, the larger of the two nations, was, on the other hand, seen as a cobwebbed, non-aligned behemoth. In 1964, Jawaharlal Nehru was replaced by Lal Bahadur Shastri, a man the US considered a nonentity. India ran low on military morale and would likely turn into an ungovernable mess. After the 1962 defeat, India was forced to abandon its outwardly non-aligned position and signed up to receive military equipment from the Soviets. Despite its impressive economic growth and India's recent defeat at the hands of China, Pakistan felt vulnerable to military threat from India, which had a much larger army. What would happen if they faced off?

This is what the players of the crisis game predicted: the war was likely to break out during August–September 1966, with Pakistan and China working hand in glove (close enough to Abdullah's intelligence which placed the war in 1965). On 31 August Pakistani forces would cross the Ceasefire Line (CFL) in Jammu and Kashmir and attack India. In the first week of September the fighting would intensify. On 6 September, Pakistani forces would capture the airfield in Srinagar and roll towards Jammu. At the same time, Chinese forces would instigate a fierce battle on the eastern border of the country.

The crisis game identified Sikkim as the point of vulnerability for India. Sikkim was a sleepy Himalayan kingdom separating India from China (erstwhile Tibet). Under a mutually agreed treaty, Sikkim was a protectorate of India, which looked after its borders and defence matters. On 6 September Chinese forces would storm into the tiny kingdom; the People's Liberation Army (PLA) would capture the capital city of Gangtok and advance further. Since Sikkim had been demanding autonomy from India for a few years, the citizens of Gangtok would be jubilant at the arrival of the Chinese army who would be hailed as liberators.[13]

Frantic diplomatic parleys involving the United States, the USSR and other nations would lead to a UN-led intervention between the warring nations. They would come to a truce with China agreeing to retreat from the Sikkim border in exchange for India handing Kashmir over to Pakistan.[14] The endgame: wresting Kashmir from India and the invasion of Sikkim, thereby negating India's position as its protector. China would establish complete supremacy over India.

~

A few months later, in 1965 itself, India and Pakistan indeed went to war; just as the pundits saw in the crystal ball that day at Arlington, a war broke out, albeit a year sooner than they had predicted.

Abdullah claimed to have informed the Indian ambassador in Algiers – with an intent to have the message relayed to the government in Delhi – about his discussion with Zhou Enlai. But his tour of Europe and his advocacy of freedom for Kashmir hadn't gone down well in Delhi. Politicians in India were demanding his arrest and the revocation of his passport. His meeting with the Chinese premier had seriously angered the government in Delhi. India's foreign minister Swaran Singh felt that Abdullah's conduct in 'seeking China's support' for Kashmir was 'highly objectionable'. Prime Minister Shastri announced that Abdullah wouldn't be allowed to visit China. The Indian intelligence agencies had been suspicious of Abdullah's meetings with the Pakistanis and Chinese. As a result of all this, the Kashmiri leader was arrested upon his arrival in India in May 1965 by Lal Bahadur Shastri's government and sent to a prison in Ootacamund, Tamil Nadu, until 1968.[15] He spent the next few years in a cycle of arrests, detentions and exiles, only to be set free in 1972.[16]

But how did the CIA get the date of the attack wrong? Why did Pakistan move against India in 1965, and not in 1966, as the CIA had earlier predicted?

After the setback against China in 1962 in which India lost around 3,250 Indian soldiers and 14,000 square miles of territory, Delhi had started to enhance its strategic capabilities and importing arms and weapons from the USSR, the US and France. The weapons from the US had arrived in 1964 and were still being inducted into India's armed forces.[17] India was spending greatly to strengthen its armed forces and budgetary outlays for defence rose from 2.1 per cent of the GNP in 1961–62 to 4.5 per cent of the GNP by 1965.[18]

India's military modernization plans included a forty-five squadron[19] air force, ten new fully equipped army mountain divisions and a million-man-strong army and a revamped navy.[20] A newly forged treaty between the Soviets and the Indians in 1964 had also led to transfer of weapons and technology to India. By 1965 the Indian army comprised 8,70,000 troops in sixteen infantry divisions. Two of the divisions were deployed in Kashmir and eight positioned along the western and eastern borders with Pakistan while six divisions were lined up on the Chinese border – a front that India was extremely wary of. Pakistan, by contrast, had a total of seven divisions stationed opposite India in West Pakistan while one division remained in East Pakistan (now Bangladesh).[21]

At the tactical level too, Rifle Factory Ishapore-manufactured 7.62 mm self-loading rifles (SLRs) were inducted into infantry units, which were a substantial improvement on the old .303 rifles used in the 1962 war. Pakistan knew that once the units familiarized themselves with these weapons, the Indian army could easily overwhelm Pakistani capability.[22]

For Pakistan it was imperative to move against India while its military overhaul and deployment of weapons and equipment was still under way. This is why the attack came earlier than anticipated. Pakistan had also been aggressively building its forces, having increased its ratio of soldiers to population from 7 per cent in 1961 to 10 per cent in 1964 (a little under a 50 per cent increase), which meant that ten out of every 100 Pakistanis were in the armed forces. The light-armed militia called the Azad Kashmir Regular Force added to their numbers. In 1963 and 1964, Pakistan had spent 3.1 per cent and 3.2 per cent of its GNP on defence respectively, but in 1965 the defence budget had jumped to 6 per cent.[23]

Another reason for attacking in 1965, instead of a year later, was that Pakistan wanted to take advantage of the political flux India was going through. Not only was India facing acute food shortage as well as a political transition after the death of Nehru who had been prime minister for seventeen long years, but also Kashmir had been on the boil for the past two years.

On a cold December morning in 1963, citizens woke up to the shocking news of the disappearance of Moi-e-Muqaddas – a sacred strand of hair believed to belong to the Prophet Muhammad – from the Hazratbal shrine in Srinagar.[24] Riots and violence tore through the state, especially targeting government property and buildings.[25] A few weeks later, after the lost relic had been recovered just as mysteriously as it had vanished, Nehru told B.N. Mullick, the intelligence chief, that Kashmir had just been saved. But the incident had unleashed the latent anger[26] festering in the Valley, which was aggravated by fear of marginalization in Hindu-majority India and incidents such as the decade-long incarceration of Sheikh Abdullah. The crisis was followed by Abdullah's release from prison in April 1964.

~

The China–Pakistan partnership showed that friendships in the subcontinent had come full circle from the day in 1959 when Pakistan's president, Ayub Khan, on a brief stopover in Delhi on the way to West Pakistan from East Pakistan, had proposed a joint India–Pakistan pact after China's invasion of Tibet.[27] At that time, Pakistan was itself engaged in a border dispute with China and Ayub Khan believed the two countries had a common enemy in China. The proposal, though, was never taken forward by India[28] as it was linked to a settlement on Kashmir favouring Pakistan.[29] Now Pakistan and China had joined hands against India.

The Chinese encouraged Ayub Khan to test India's mettle in case of an all-out war and prodded him to conduct a dress rehearsal. In June 1965, Pakistani forces advanced towards Indian posts in the Rann of Kutch on India's western border. Pakistan rolled out its newly acquired American Patton tanks and artillery to take on Indian forward positions. The skirmish was brief, but Pakistan displayed superior armour mobility and effective use of artillery. Both sides agreed to a ceasefire on 30 June 1965, but in the ensuing stalemate, Pakistan achieved an edge over India. By then, Ayub Khan and the Pakistani government were convinced that India lacked the political will and military capability to wage a protracted war.

Ayub Khan was a general who had attended the Sandhurst military academy in England before India's partition. Among his batchmates were officers who later joined the Indian army, including the Indian military chief in the 1965 war – General Jayanto Nath Chaudhuri – his company mate at Sandhurst. Fond of whisky and horses, the anglicized Ayub wore pinstriped suits and smoked a pipe. He was urbane and sophisticated. Apparently, when he was served pork ribs during a personal visit to President Lyndon Johnson's ranch in Texas in 1961[30] he ignored the misstep for the sake of diplomacy. Yet prejudice seemed to have coloured Ayub's thinking in the years around the war, causing him to infamously remark that 'the Hindu had no stomach for a fight'[31] and could be silenced with a few good blows.

Ayub Khan and his foreign minister, Zulfikar Ali Bhutto, were believed to be proponents of the theory of 'civilizational supremacy'. For centuries, invaders rained attacks on India from the north and west, overrunning the local forces that stood in their way. Even after Independence, India and Indians continued to be seen as a land and a people inherently vulnerable to foreign attacks and aggression.

Unlike the president, Bhutto had neither shared dormitories with Indians nor trained alongside them. His thinking was shaped by bitter personal memories from Partition. Bhutto's father used to be a minister (or dewan) in the princely province of Junagadh in Gujarat. At the time of Partition, the Nawab of Junagadh wanted to join Pakistan. Unhappy at being pressured by India to join the union, he decided to drive to the airfield (taking his dogs along) and fly to Pakistan in his aircraft.

A young Bhutto and his parents moved to Pakistan as well. The memory of being uprooted from Jamnagar embittered him towards India forever. He espoused the idea of infiltrating irregular forces into Kashmir, even managing to convince Ayub Khan, who otherwise preferred classical military operations. Bhutto would go on to be involved in two successive wars with India within six years.

Kashmir had been an obsession for the Pakistani leadership since the nation's independence in 1947, even at the risk of losing friends in the international community. This seemed to be the perfect moment to wrest the vale of Kashmir from India, forever.

In August 1965, seven Pakistani guerrilla teams[32] sneaked into the Kashmir Valley under the cover of a moonless night to launch Operation Gibraltar. The teams were named Ghaznavi, Babur, Salahuddin, Nusrat, Tariq, Qasim, Khalid and K Force, most of them named after victorious generals from Islamic folklore.[33] The aim was to fan a local uprising in the Valley. Infiltrating columns were divided into groups of 300 to 400 men consisting of Pakistani army soldiers and trained militia.

Gibraltar was an unusual code name for a military operation in the Kashmir Valley in India. It was inspired from the eighth-century Umayyad conquest of Hispania, launched from Gibraltar. The Umayyads were a Muslim army of the Umayyad Caliphate who invaded the Christian Visigothic kingdom located on the Iberian peninsula in Hispania (the Iberian peninsula is part of modern-day Spain and Portugal). The Muslim army would bring the Christian Iberian peninsula under their control in a successful military campaign.

Clearly, Pakistan was attempting to invoke and stake claim over a storied Islamic legacy.

Coming back to Operation Gibraltar, on that August night in 1965, the aforementioned groups of men stole past the CFL,[34] shawls covering their faces. The next morning, five policemen lay dead, their bodies riddled with bullets, their eyes open and mouths agape. By the next day, more incidents of plundering and death were reported. No war had broken out on the front. Yet, mysteriously, people were dying everywhere. Vehicles were ambushed, offices were attacked, army garrisons were fired upon and Indian soldiers were killed. The infiltrators declared on radio that Kashmir was now free. The Chinese premier Zhou Enlai and his generals had used guerrilla tactics against rival Kuomintang forces. Operation Gibraltar was Pakistan's chance to employ the same to make Kashmir implode. The guerrillas were regular Pakistani paramilitary forces trained and armed by the Chinese.[35]

It had taken three years for India to restore the right military leadership and shake off a culture of complacency and nepotism post the 1962 defeat. The beginnings of such a change in operations of the Indian army began to be felt in the 1965 war. Lieutenant General Harbaksh Singh was one of the military leaders to lead the revival. Leading the war on the western front, Harbaksh saw Pakistani aggression as an opportunity to launch an offensive to capture the heights of the Haji Pir pass inside Pakistan and close down lines of infiltration. In a daring surgical operation, para commandos led by Major Rajinder Singh Dayal captured the Haji Pir pass on 28 August. Within less than a month of its launch, Operation Gibraltar had collapsed. The Indian army's

Indian soldiers capture Haji Pir pass in the 1965 war.

response had been swift and Kashmiris, contrary to Bhutto and Ayub's assumptions, had not supported the infiltrators. Instead, they helped the army nab the infiltrators, whom they saw as outsiders.[36] Because the Pakistani infiltrators hadn't planned well and didn't speak the local dialect, they stood out. Operation Gibraltar proved to be a disaster.[37] The infiltrators were captured and several Chinese-made weapons and grenades were recovered. They also revealed they had been trained by the People's Liberation Army.

While Operation Gibraltar had failed, it was time for Pakistan to launch the bigger, more conventional strike. The road that connected Jammu to places in Kashmir such as Naushera, Rajouri and Poonch lay over the Akhnur bridge. Pakistan's best chances lay in capturing Jammu and Akhnur, thereby cutting off Kashmir from the rest of the country. The shortest distance from Pakistan to Akhnur was via Chhamb in Jammu and Kashmir.[38] The

Ministry of Defence

Pakistani infiltrators in Operation Gibraltar captured
in Indian territory in August 1965.

pompously named Operation Grand Slam announced itself one morning with Patton tanks thunderously rolling into the village of Chhamb Jaurian. Two Pakistani regiments with Patton tanks ominously charged towards Akhnur[39] to sever Kashmir from the rest of India. Major General Akhtar Hassan Malik's forces initially surprised the Indian defence and made a serious thrust across the Manawi river in the Chhamb Jaurian area. The fall of Akhnur seemed imminent. This was exactly what Ayub had wanted: a quick war, with rapid armour movement and capture. Then, Pakistan inexplicably changed the commanders while waiting to mount an attack on Akhnur, which they were poised to capture. Major General Akhtar Malik, the architect of the advance, was controversially replaced with a favourite of President Ayub Khan – Major General Yahya Khan. Several reasons were given for this, one being that the replacement was a preplanned move to bring Malik to the headquarters. Another was that Malik had overstretched the communication line and so the Pakistani army chief needed Malik to return and establish control from the rear headquarters. Ayub Khan was sure of victory and wanted his protégé Yahya to helm the historic moment. The change in commanders resulted in a twenty-four-hour delay in Pakistan's offensive, by which time the Indians were able to bring in reinforcements. The Indian forces, led by the irrepressible Harbaksh, bravely outfought Pakistan's superior US-made Patton tanks and C-104 aircrafts with their Second-World-War-vintage Centurion tanks and Gnat fighter planes.[40]

Capitalizing on this favourable turn of events, Lal Bahadur Shastri decided to launch a diversionary attack. India had done the unexpected and expanded the theatre of war – a move that neither envisaged by the crisis game nor indicated by the Rann of Kutch skirmish.

On 6 September, Indian troops attacked Pakistani positions in Punjab, leaving key cities such as Lahore vulnerable to air attacks. Confrontations ensued in which the battle of Asal Uttar witnessed the biggest tank battles since the Second World War. After India's offensive, Pakistan's rampaging forces managed to capture the town of Khem Karan and were expected to advance

Indian Air Force scrambling a Gnat for an air attack in 1965.

further. However, India's 4 Mountain Division was waiting for them with a surprise innovatively prepared by Brigadier Thomas K. Theograj – one of several military commanders who played critical, yet unsung, roles in changing the course of the war on ground.

The division had withdrawn to assume a horseshoe defensive position around the sugarcane fields in the Asal Uttar area. Next morning, when the M-47 and M-48 Patton tanks rolled into the fields, the swampy ground slowed down their advance and many were stuck in the slush. The Pakistani forces realized they had been lured inside a horseshoe trap. Ninety-nine Pakistani tanks, mostly Pattons, and a few Shermans and Chaffees, were destroyed or captured in a ferocious counteroffensive by Indian forces. The Pakistani general, Major General Nasir Ahmed Khan, was killed in the battle. India's Colonel Salim Caleb, in command of the cavalry regiment, displayed exemplary courage and inspiring leadership, spurring his men to destroy fifteen Pakistani tanks and capturing nine.

The battle of Asal Uttar, literally meaning 'the befitting response', greatly tilted the scales in favour of India. Interestingly, a young lieutenant, Pervez Musharraf, who fought in the historic battle of Asal Uttar, would go on to become the president of his country many years later.[41] The site of the battle was littered with tanks that couldn't be moved. A town was thus born, called Patton Nagar – a graveyard for the tanks once used by Pakistani forces.

After this victory India redoubled its resolve and decided to attack the Lahore and Sialkot sectors simultaneously. The Indian forces were led by dogged battlefield commanders such as Colonel (later Brigadier) Desmond Hayde who led the forces across the tough Ichhogil canal that had been built by Pakistan to protect Lahore in case of a war.[42] Pakistan, lacking geographical depth, stood to lose major cities if the conflict continued any longer. The town of Dograi, which had to be won to reach Lahore after the canal was breached, was an important one for the defender.

When Ayub Khan had originally shared his plans of the attack with Zhou Enlai, the Chinese leader had told him to be prepared for a long war and to be ready to lose cities in order to win overall. 'Be prepared to lose Lahore,' the Chinese leader had told him.[43] But Ayub had planned for a short war. Zhou Enlai's words would prove prophetic within a few days.

By 21 September, Indian forces had reached the outskirts of Lahore and Sialkot. Pakistan wasn't about to give up the critical defence of Dograi. Shortly after midnight on 22 September, the Indian army made a blistering advance against the defending Pakistani forces, which culminated in the battle of Dograi, one of the bloodiest battles in Indian history. It began with firing on both sides and ended with clashes of bayonets and hand-to-hand fights. Indian forces managed to wipe out the Pakistani defence and captured Dograi. They were now knocking on the doors of Lahore. For Pakistan, the war clearly hadn't gone according to plan.

Ayub's misplaced belief in his military supremacy had been proved wrong. On top of this obvious logical fallacy, he had also mistakenly perceived the Indian army as an army of Hindu soldiers. Ranjit Singh Dayal, who led the capture of the Haji Pir pass, was a Jat Sikh, as was Lieutenant General Harbaksh who led India in the 1965 war. General J.N. Chaudhuri, the chief of the army, was a Bengali Hindu. Salim Caleb, the young cavalry commander, was a Christian. One of the brightest stars of the war, Abdul Hamid, was also a Muslim who worked as a tailor before joining the Indian army. As the company quartermaster havildar, Hamid's primary job was to ensure supplies to troops.[44] In an unprecedented individual action in the history of war, Hamid single-handedly destroyed seven Pakistani tanks.[45] The Keelor brothers, the first siblings to win Vir Chakras for their heroics using a Gnat fighter to bring down superior Sabre jets, were Christians as was their Wing Commander, William Goodman. Colonel Adi Tarapore was a Parsi officer whose exploits, before he died fighting for his

Ministry of Defence

Defence Minister Chavan with troops after the battle of
Dograi that brought them close to Lahore.

armoured regiment, so moved the Pakistani forces that
they stopped shelling during his cremation as a mark of
respect.[46] Desmond Hayde, who was born to English
parents but stayed back after 1947 and joined the Indian
army, was called the bawra Jat (the crazy Jat). He led his
battalion across the Icchogil canal to lay the beachhead
for the Indian assault into Lahore. Ayub's army had been
thwarted by the combined strength of a secular India.

~

As soon as India launched the diversionary attack in Pakistani Punjab, the Chinese came out with a statement condemning India and warning the Indian government 'that it must bear responsibility for all the consequences of its criminal and extended aggression'.

As Indian forces pressed towards Lahore, help for Pakistan arrived from China, that had forcibly occupied Tibet since 1950. 1 September 1965 turned out to be a crucial date in the plan against India. While Pakistan launched Operation Grand Slam and their tanks rolled into India, China announced the creation of the Tibet Autonomous Region (TAR). This decision instantly organized areas of Tibet, like Amdo and Kham, into Chinese provinces. This move strengthened China's growing administrative control over Tibet. A week later, on 8 September, China issued a warning to India about building military structures on Chinese soil in the newly established TAR. In the past few years, the Chinese had occasionally complained about Indian military incursions across the border, but the early September warning that year was a forerunner to its plot related to Sikkim.

On 17 September, at 6 a.m., a messenger woke up India's defence minister, Y.B. Chavan,[47] who had been occupied with the war with Pakistan on the western front. A note arrived from Peking: China had served an ultimatum to India, giving it three days to dismantle its alleged bunkers inside the TAR. Lal Bahadur Shastri denied the allegations, stressed that the defence structures, built on the Sikkim side of the border in September 1962, had been abandoned in November the same year.[48] He even offered to conduct a joint review of the border. China's real motive was to break India's momentum against Pakistan and disable its ability to pull out troops from the Sino-Indian border for the ongoing war in the west.

China had begun to amass troops against India at the border along Sikkim, similar to the move in the crisis game. It appeared that the war had, after a stutter, reverted to the script of Arlington.

2

In the Shadow of the Dragon: The War Moves East

In mid-August, much before the focus of the 1965 war moved east, standing at the edge of Sikkim's northern border with Tibet, now part of China, Sagat Singh stared at the desolate mountains that stretched before him. The tranquillity on the border struck him as odd. Through his binoculars he could not see any movement among the Chinese soldiers. Around him stood a handful of his own infantrymen manning the post in their new winter fatigues, which Sagat had managed to procure along with more than ten tonnes of defence stores after an uphill struggle against red tape. But all this was about to change. The relative calm belied what was already happening behind the scenes.

On the border, at the edge of Sikkim's northern shelf, is a significant pass, a gap in the mountains, which has been silent witness to histories of traders, Hindu and Buddhist pilgrims, the journey undertaken by the Dalai Lama. The Tibetans call it the Pass of Listening Ear.[1] It is also called the Nathu La pass. On either side of the pass soldiers managed surrogate lands: Sikkim was India's protectorate, while China had occupied Tibet.

Three years before China occupied Tibet, at the time of India's partition in 1947, when the rulers of India's princely states were deciding whether to join India or Pakistan, Palden Thondup, the prince of Sikkim, had rushed to India's prime minister, Jawaharlal Nehru, in Delhi, seeking autonomy for his state.[2] Nehru had promised a special status for Sikkim, despite opposition from Sardar Vallabhbhai Patel who wanted to integrate Sikkim into the Indian union. But in 1950, China's moves in Tibet scared Sikkim right into India's waiting arms. Tashi Namgyal, the king, or Chogyal, of Sikkim, signed a treaty with India[3] to become an Indian protectorate[4] on 12 December 1950.

The treaty gave Sikkim autonomy in its internal affairs while India was in charge of its foreign affairs and defence matters. In the years that followed, however, India's influence in Sikkim grew as Indian bureaucrats and civil servants sent to Sikkim as political officers had a persuasive voice within the state's administration.[5] Along with the bureaucrats, the Indian army's 17 Division had been stationed in Sikkim along the Chinese border, with its headquarters at Gangtok. Lieutenant General Harbaksh, who was leading the army in the war in 1965, had commanded that division in the past. The division now had a new commander – Major General Sagat Singh.

Sagat Singh, the division commander.

The 3,488-kilometre Sino-Indian border was at its kindest at Jelep La and Nathu La.[6] In the 1962 war, no one fired a shot here. The border dispute between India and China then involved other areas such as North East Frontier Agency (NEFA) and at Aksai Chin. In 1962, Lieutenant General Harbaksh Singh had ordered an army deployment in the Tukla area, facing Jelep La, and also at Chhanggu (Tsomgo), covering the approach from Nathu La to Gangtok. Border outposts continued to hold the passes at Nathu La and Jelep La. Another force held its position near the capital city of Gangtok. Under Harbaksh's leadership, a strong defensive firewall was built. The Chinese chose not to attack on the Sikkim axis, ostensibly since Sikkim was still an independent associate state of India, that China was keen to cultivate politically.

In the 1962 war, there was a short period when Indian forces fared better: when Lieutenant General Brij Mohan Kaul, who was the commander of 4 Corps, reported sick and had to be replaced by Harbaksh. In the brief period that Harbaksh was in charge, there was no further loss of territory.[7] Subsequently, Kaul recovered and was reinstated. The trail of disasters resumed. Like Harbaksh, there were other competent military leaders who did not get an opportunity to participate in the 1962 war. One of them was Sagat Singh. In the 1962 war, Harbaksh was the commander of 33 Corps, based in Siliguri in West Bengal, under whose command lay 17 Mountain Division in Sikkim. In the summer of 1965, Sagat arrived to take over the same division.

Sometime in the early 1960s, an American couple visiting the Taj Mahal in Agra on a holiday happened to meet Sagat at the city's Clarks Shiraz hotel. They had been to Lisbon earlier and recalled seeing Sagat's face on a poster in the city. The poster promised a reward of $10,000 to anyone who would bring the head of the Indian army officer Sagat Singh.[8] After India gained independence in 1947, Portugal, the last remaining European colonial occupier, still retained three enclaves in India, including Goa, the largest one, covering 3,635 square kilometres. But the winds of freedom couldn't be kept out of Goa for long. On 15 August 1955, the Portuguese-controlled police of Goa fired on a group of independence protesters there, causing several deaths, an incident that set off a frenzy of protests and angry political statements and rallies.[9] Things finally came to a head when an Indian ship was fired on, resulting in the death of an engineer on board.

Portugal was unmoved by the violence, forcing Prime Minister Jawaharlal Nehru to take military action. On 29 November 1961, Brigadier Sagat received a call from the director of military operations. He was asked to lead his parachute brigade for the attack to liberate Goa. This mission was codenamed Operation Vijay and it used a two-pronged approach.[10]

Sagat was given the responsibility of leading a parachute brigade from the northern flank. The previous night, All India Radio had announced, rather indiscreetly, that the Indian army was moving into Goa. Fearing that they may have lost the element of surprise, Sagat decided to advance faster than expected. He moved the para brigade before 17 Division could move into Goa. Sagat's troops crossed the Mandovi river and advanced to the capital city of Panjim, which was soon captured and the Portuguese forces overpowered.

While Sagat had distinguished himself in Goa in 1961, his preference for bold military thinking and defying traditional tactics in operations made him unpopular. In an Indian army dominated by a bureaucratic and often circumspect mindset as displayed in the 1962 war, conformism was the norm, and departures in decision-making were frowned upon. Sagat's feisty and innovative style,[11] and his penchant for speed and surge, stood out. His Portuguese enemies continued to remember him on the walls of Lisbon.

A year after the action in Goa, when India went to war with China, Sagat and his brigade were kept waiting in the sidelines.[12] The orders never arrived and Sagat sat out the war, a major loss for India.

~

Upon arriving in mid-August 1965 as commander of the 17 Division in the hills of Sikkim, Sagat decided to travel to remote infantry posts along the border, sometimes walking for days to reach troop detachments on lonely ridges. The newly appointed general was a keen horseman too. He would frequently ride along with his aide de camp to visit soldiers living in inhospitable forward posts. He would also take helicopters to cover places that were far away. The forty-six-year-old general was busy learning the lay of the land. The peace in the mountains also enabled him to attend to the inadequate stores and clothing of the battalions in remote posts close to Cho La, another pass on the border between Sikkim and China.

In early September 1965, inputs began to pour in from the border posts that the Chinese PLA could be seen amassing troops at bunkers along Sikkim's border. Soon scores of armed soldiers had filled the area that had hitherto remained calm and peaceful. The stretches of desolate, wildly beautiful land opening out into the Yatung valley in Tibet that Sagat had watched with wonderment were now filled with busy, uniformed men from the PLA. The men arrived in trucks carrying weapons, backpacks, tents and communication sets and started digging trenches and settling into their bunkers. The message was stark: any further moves by India against Pakistan in the west would be met with harsh retribution. In line with the predictions of the crisis game, China was willing to attack India through Sikkim in the east.

~

As mentioned at the end of the previous chapter, on 17 September China sent an ultimatum to India giving it three days to dismantle fifty-six alleged incursions into Tibet. Half an hour after he had been rudely woken up by the messenger carrying the ultimatum, Yashwantrao Chavan, India's defence minister, tuned in to All India Radio. His fears were confirmed. The messenger was right. China had indeed issued the menacing threat to India.

Chavan drove to Prime Minister Shastri's residence where the prime minister held a two-hour-long emergency committee[13] meeting to discuss the new threat. The warning unnerved the Indian leadership. The ultimatum also accused India of illegally occupying 92,000 square kilometres of territory in NEFA (current-day Arunachal Pradesh). In 1962, when the two countries fought a border war, amongst the major territorial disputes was China's territorial claim on Indian land in NEFA. China's contention stemmed from its belief that historical ties existed between the Tawang monastery in Arunachal Pradesh and the Lhasa monastery in Tibet, that had already been claimed by China. China considered Arunachal as part of south Tibet. China was now raking up the old issue again.

Pressing on the mood of panic and dread that had begun to grip the Indian government, the warning from Peking ended on a condescending note. 'India must bear the responsibility for all the consequences arising therefrom,' the Chinese threatened.[14] The Chinese note had changed the equation for India. The veil had been lifted: the old nemesis had decided to plainly enter the war.

India decided that a proposal for a joint investigation of the alleged bunkers in Tibet be put forward. (But the Chinese would go on to reject the proposal.) Later that day, India also reached out to the US, the USSR and Great Britain for help. Chavan also took to the radio to assuage a concerned nation that while a large-scale Chinese attack was not anticipated, given their movement in the northeast there could indeed be a diversionary attack there.

Following the script of the crisis game, the West was

getting entangled in the conflict at this point because of the SOS from India. The White House swung into action and asked the CIA for an estimate on the credibility of China's threat and what its next moves would be. The CIA assessed that China 'will avoid direct, large-scale military involvement in the Indo-Pakistani war' but that 'there is an even chance it will make small scale military probes across the Indian frontier'.[15] The CIA assessment emphasized China's intent to intimidate the Indian leadership politically and militarily.[16] But US President Lyndon Johnson didn't want to enter the war as he was occupied with his own Vietnam war at that time.

The Soviets, worried that China was harbouring plans to convert India into a satellite state, were concerned about the potential loss of their influence. They planned to supply weapons to India during the war.[17] By now the UN was also involved and the discussions to establish peace had begun to move at a frenetic pace.

In the face of international scrutiny, China decided to pin the blame of the India–Pakistan war on India. 'The whole world now sees that it was India which launched a war of aggression against Pakistan, thus endangering peace in Asia and the world, and that it was China and other justice-upholding countries which by their firm anti-aggressive stand punctured your aggressive arrogance,' a Chinese ministry for external affairs would declare falsely and patronizingly.[18]

As the three-day deadline drew closer and the world's attention was on China, Peking extended the deadline by another three days. Meanwhile on the western front, Pakistan was running out of defensive military options, since India was approaching Lahore with its larger attacking force that could sustain the war.

Islamabad was still hopeful that the US would take its side against a Soviet-backed India and provide diplomatic support in the war. However, Walter McConaughy, the US ambassador in Islamabad, received a clear message for Bhutto from the American state department: 'We must view India's attacks across the Pakistani border in over-all context of events in the past few weeks. It is clear from the UN Secretary General's report that immediate crisis began with substantial infiltration of armed men from the Pakistan side.'[19] Four days after Indian forces successfully entered Pakistani Punjab, McConaughy asked Bhutto to consider a ceasefire proposal to safeguard the territory of Pakistan.

An irate Bhutto shot back at McConaughy, saying that Pakistanis would sell all their possessions and family heirlooms to repulse the Indian occupation of Kashmir and free the state from India.

McConaughy told Bhutto in that meeting that Pakistan was responsible for the war with India, and had wrongly used US weapons meant to be deployed against communist China against India. Frustrated at not getting support from the US, Pakistan, its back against the wall, was desperate for China to step into the war in the next three days.

A comeback plan was hatched.

On 19 September 1965, two public figures quietly boarded a chartered plane bound for China from Pakistan. They slipped away like renegades in the night. Their mission was critical for their nation. They were Pakistani president, Ayub Khan, and his foreign minister, Zulfikar Ali Bhutto.

In Peking, the duo met with Zhou Enlai and Marshal Chen Yi for long discussions. The Pakistani leaders had come prepared to bring up the issue of Pakistan's difficulties in the face of India's numerical superiority of forces. They wanted China's intervention at the earliest against India. Marshal Chen Yi, having heard them at the meeting, could only offer terse advice. He told the Pakistanis not to give up, even if they lost some large cities in the process. Marshal Chen Yi assured Ayub Khan of China's support in such an eventuality. Zhou believed that in a long-drawn-out war, India's numbers would be neutralized and the will of the Indian people – believed to be against a long confrontation – would flounder. China's ultimatums to Delhi were part of an attrition strategy – keeping India guessing.

Ayub Khan had planned for a short, quick war, which was now threatening to extend beyond Pakistan's military means. The blustering Pakistani president had neither the heart to fight nor the means to see it through. Ayub had panicked and made the hasty trip to China because his army, short on ammunition, had run out of options. The duo returned home empty-handed. With the international community coming out in favour of Delhi, and with the Indian army at Lahore's gates, Delhi now held the diplomatic and military advantage.

In India, a decision was made at a meeting on 20 September that Shastri held with his defence minister, Y.B. Chavan, and the army chief, General J.N. Chaudhuri. Chavan, who maintained a diary of the war, made an entry that day: 'After some preliminary discussion about the military point of view, it was agreed that Prime Minister should send to [UN Secretary General] U Thant ... (a message), confirming our willingness to order simple ceasefire if Pakistan is agreeable.'[20] Like clockwork, on 22 September, the UNSC voted unanimously and demanded that India and Pakistan accept a ceasefire and revert to their pre-war position of 6 August.

According to another version, General Chaudhuri had advised the prime minister to agree to a ceasefire, citing inadequacy of frontline ammunition. Several historians later decried the decision as wrong since only 14 per cent ammunition had been expended in the war. India had held the tactical advantage of occupying Pakistani territory close to its major cities such as Lahore and Sialkot. However, it was collectively felt by India's political leadership that it was far from achieving a spectacular victory. Instead, a ceasefire was thought to advocate India's intent to establish peace and thereby increase chances of securing post-war gains through diplomacy.

On closer analysis, it was China's belligerence that led India to accept the ceasefire in spite of its position of military advantage over Pakistan.

Ayub Khan agreed to the ceasefire on 22 September, the extended deadline set by the Chinese in their ultimatum – which turned out to be a calculated deception aimed to coerce India and influence its actions during the war, such as keeping in check India's ambitions to capture key cities such as Lahore during the offensive movement into Pakistan. This was proved because after the ceasefire the Chinese announced that Indian troops had withdrawn their military structures, which had never existed in the first place, from Chinese territory.[21]

With India and Pakistan agreeing to a ceasefire, the focus shifted eastwards, setting the stage for a tussle in the forgotten passes of the mountain kingdom of Sikkim.

3

Protests, Disagreements and a Temporary Truce: Advantage China

August–September 1965 turned out to be a season of disquiet marked by armies challenging boundaries, politicians trying to instigate dissidents and infiltrators breaching borders.

It was also a season of heightened diplomatic sensitivities and brittle India–China bilateral relations as can be seen by an incident that took place on 27 August,[1] while India was fighting off Pakistani infiltrators in Kashmir. China had made a perplexing allegation that 800 sheep and fifty-nine yaks that had crossed over into India[2] along with their herdsmen had actually been stolen by Indian troops from the Tibetan herdsmen

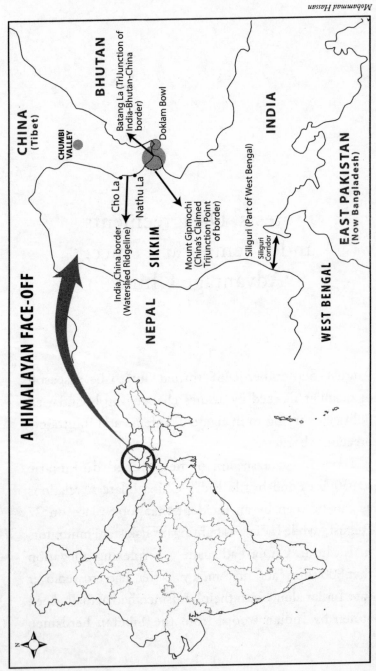

A HIMALAYAN FACE-OFF

CHINA
(Tibet)

BHUTAN

CHUMBI
VALLEY

Batang La (Trijunction of
India-Bhutan-China
border)

Doklam Bowl

Cho La

Nathu La

India-China border
(Watershed Ridgeline)

Mount Gipmochi
(China's Claimed
Trijunction Point
of border)

SIKKIM

NEPAL

INDIA

Siliguri (Part of West Bengal)

Siliguri
Corridor

EAST PAKISTAN
(Now Bangladesh)

WEST BENGAL

N

This map is not to scale and is for explanatory purposes only. The international boundaries on the maps of India are neither purported to be correct nor authentic by Survey of India directives.

close to the Sikkim border. No one would have given the incident a ghost of a chance of pushing an already delicate relationship to the edge.

Such border crossings were not unusual. Earlier that year, on 29 May, two Tibetan women named Damque and Jitzongm[3] disappeared from a place called Khampa Dzong in Tibet, close to the Sikkim border. Sensing an opportunity to escape from China-occupied Tibet, the women had in fact crossed the border and reached Sikkim. Unsure and terrified, they went to the Indian police and complained about the miserable living conditions in Tibet and sought asylum in India. The Chinese, however, had a different version of the story and accused Indians of abducting the women.

The allegation about the stolen animals evoked considerable mirth in India. China demanded the animals be returned along with the four 'missing' shepherds. India denied knowledge about the livestock or the men. The ministry of external affairs issued a statement that Indian troops had not kidnapped any Tibetans nor seized any livestock. The statement read: 'If the Tibetans with sheep and yaks had indeed crossed over, they were free to return if they desired to do so.'[4] China continued to threaten India with a repeat of 1962 if the livestock weren't returned. Peking threatened India with war at every small opportunity. A light-hearted response was perhaps the only possible answer to the ludicrous allegation and war threat.

On 24 September, a forty-two-year-old Indian politician from the opposition decided to take matters into his own self-assured hands. He gathered a band of protesters and drove to the Chinese embassy in Delhi. Atal Bihari Vajpayee, the young politician known for his wit and sharp mind, was at the forefront of a flock of 800 sheep.[5] The protesters stood before the Chinese embassy, flashing placards with the slogan: 'Eat me but save the world!'

Annoyed at the sight of the sea of white sheep, the embassy staffers complained that the protesters were 'a mob of Indian hooligans whose mischievous agitation was supported by the Indian government'. China's ministry of foreign affairs issued an irate note to the Indian embassy in Peking,[6] complaining that Indians were making a din that 'China wants to start a world war over some sheep and a few yaks'. The note reiterated: 'You must return every single one of the border inhabitants and livestock you kidnapped and seized from Chinese territory across the China–Sikkim border.'

The note continued: 'The Indian Government will definitely not succeed in its attempt, by staging this ugly anti-Chinese farce, to cover up its crimes of aggression against China and the wretched picture of its troops fleeing in panic.'[7] The Chinese signed off on a condescending note: 'The Indian troops who had intruded into the Chinese side of the China–Sikkim boundary could not but flee helter skelter under the surveillance of Chinese troops.'

The quirky humour behind Vajpayee's brilliant protest was lost in the inane exchanges of the two governments. India objected to China's comments on the protest and alleged that Peking was interfering in India's internal affairs, even taking a swipe at the lack of political freedom in China by saying that Indians enjoyed the right to express themselves.

The acrimonious exchange wasn't about to end as India referred to Tibet in one of its notes, suddenly appearing both unusually blunt and brave: 'The Chinese Government appears to have been embarrassed ... that there are not four but thousands of Tibetans who have left their homeland and taken refuge in India. But that is a fact, though not a creditable one for the Chinese regime in Tibet. The Chinese note has stated that these ... Tibetan refugees are a debt which India owes to China. On the contrary, it is a debt which China owes to the people of Tibet for making it impossible for them to live in freedom and dignity in their own motherland.'[8] The Indians didn't hold back from calling the Chinese occupation of Tibet an invasion,[9] and even brought up the Dalai Lama, a very sore topic for the Chinese.

Four decades later, Vajpayee became India's prime minister. The young protester of 1965 then visited China in 2003 and succeeded in thawing relations and reopening the trade route from Sikkim via the Nathu La pass.[10]

The year 1965, however, presented a completely different scenario when India and China's relations were dominated by openly hostile exchanges between bureaucrats on both sides. Given the rising bitterness of the exchanges it was no surprise when PLA troops began to quietly make their way to a border mountain in Sikkim, their focus on another sleepy, beautiful pass on the Sikkim–Tibet border. The gentle pass was so even, it was called 'the lovely level pass' in the local dialect or, simply, Jelep La.

Jelep La was historically used by traders, soldiers, refugees and travellers alike to move between Sikkim and Tibet. Trade flourished as caravans from Kalimpong, West Bengal, regularly made their way to the markets in Lhasa, Tibet. But when the big war broke out in 1962, Jelep La was shut down. During the war, a Chinese attack loomed large and Indian troops, stationed at the pass, were ready. The fighting happened elsewhere while the pass, like Nathu La, continued to be held by Indian troops.

After 1962, Jelep La was almost forgotten except by Indian forward detachments that sat guarding it. It began to be referred to as the Lonely Pass. In the fall of 1965, with the arrival of Chinese troops along the Tibet–Sikkim border, the Lonely Pass transformed into a hub of activity once again.

Much of the attention during the war with Pakistan in September that year had been focused on the build-up of forces at Nathu La, the pass to Jelep La's west. However, a quiet build-up was taking place at Jelep La as well.

As war raged along the western borders of India, the PLA rapidly increased its presence along both Jelep La and Nathu La. Two Indian mountain divisions were positioned near the passes; 17 Mountain Division covered the territory opposite Nathu La, 27 Mountain Division guarded the area opposite Jelep La. Border outposts of the divisions held the two passes. The two divisions came under the Indian army's 33 Corps, which, headquartered in Siliguri, about 160 kilometres from Nathu La, was responsible for the security of the region.

Around the time the war with Pakistan broke out that year, Lieutenant General G.G. Bewoor, the corps commander, called an important meeting in Siliguri with his division commanders, which included a newly appointed Major General Sagat Singh. The senior officers discussed contingency plans and the actions expected of the Indian army in the event of an escalation in hostilities with China along the border.

A staff officer in Sagat's team at the division

headquarters in Gangtok recalled that when the corps' operational plan of response to hostilities was made, the corps commander had the assent of both division commanders – Major Generals Sagat Singh and Harcharan Singh.[11] It was agreed that in case of hostilities, troops would vacate the forward positions at Nathu La and Jelep La and occupy defensive positions, further away from the border, lower down the slope at Chhanggu and Lungthu in Sikkim. In the event of an imminent Chinese offensive, Indian troops would withdraw to their positions seven to nine miles deep inside Indian territory. The plan was to consolidate the troops and fight from a stronger defensive position, instead of obtaining a thinner forward line. Brigadier Lakhpat Singh, then a staff officer to Sagat, later commented that the plan 'looked absurd and stupid'[12] as it violated the cardinal principle of defence, which was to continually track an enemy's movement and maintain visual or surveillance contact, lacking which the defender was left groping for a response based on speculation.

Over 5000 Chinese troops were deployed opposite Nathu La and Jelep La, which were held by the Indian army at that time. Elsewhere, along the Line of Actual Control (LAC) that served as the border between India and China, minor skirmishes had erupted, highlighting China's growing audacity to attack isolated Indian patrols or forward posts. On 19 September 1965, Chinese army patrols crossed over the LAC[13] in Tsaskur in the western sector near Ladakh and killed three Indian policemen whom they had abducted. Encouraged by their success, on 20 September, Chinese soldiers crossed the Donchui La pass on the Sikkim–Tibet border to ambush and kidnap three Indian soldiers, as stated by G.S. Bajpai in *China's Shadow Over Sikkim*.

The Chinese attacks had made everyone from the battalions to the corps headquarters in Siliguri quite tense. Orders were given to lay minefields on the likely future approaches of the Chinese soldiers. The 11th Battalion of Jammu & Kashmir Rifles (11 Jak Rif) was a newly raised battalion, which had taken over defences at Cho La pass in Sikkim at 16,000 feet in July 1965.[14] One night, a minelaying party under Second Lieutenant Raman Bakshi of 11 Jak Rif set out in the dark. The weather worsened and the rains made the going slippery. During the laying of an M16 mine, young Raman met with an accident and lost his life, becoming the first martyr of the 1965 war on the Chinese front.[15]

The PLA troops gathered along the border now made increasingly aggressive demonstrations in front of the Indian defences positioned at Nathu La and Cho La. On 17 September they had accused India of disturbing peace on the border. That day, two officers,

Lieutenant Bhandral of 11 Jak Rif at Cho La and Captain V.N. Thapar of 17 Marathas at Nathu La, reported large PLA units advancing with weapons towards the passes. Chinese forces marched from the Chumbi valley, stealthily moving in a tactical formation, crossing bounds of a few hundred feet before halting and then moving ahead again.[16] On the Indian side, the troops stood guard.

The Indian army stood its ground and withheld firing as the instructions were clear: avoid escalation of the situation, which was what the Chinese wanted. The Chinese were keen to maintain an upper hand by engaging and attacking Indian troops in skirmishes, on grounds of their choosing. Alongside such pinprick attacks, they constantly brought up reminders of 1962 and the lessons for India. The headquarters at Siliguri were following the developments closely.

As the Chinese began to amass additional forces opposite the passes and heightened the pressure on India at the border,[17] orders from 33 Corps came in for 17 and 27 Divisions to vacate Nathu La and Jelep La, and occupy positions in depth. The plan was to avoid engaging China, even if it meant sacrificing two crucial passes at the border. There were no orders to evict from other areas, including Cho La, since Indians expected the Chinese line of advance to be through Nathu La and Jelep La. The McMahon Line,[18] which India considered its international border with China, followed the watershed principle. A watershed is a basin-like land form defined by high points that descends into lower elevations and stream valleys. A watershed line is formed by a continuous ridgeline that separates two distinct areas of land where a common set of streams and rivulets drain into a single larger body of water, such as a larger river. Water poured on any part of the watershed would naturally run off into a common deepest point. The border passes of Nathu La, Cho La and Jelep La, between Sikkim and China, were long, narrow watersheds. The Chinese, who had never accepted the McMahon Line as the border, implicitly expected India to avoid a tense stand-off and retreat from the two passes on the watershed line – Nathu La and Jelep La.

The Indian army had planned to fight the battle from defensive positions deeper inside own territory if the Chinese forces came in from Nathu La and Jelep La. But what if the Chinese plan was not to advance beyond the passes but simply to occupy them? The Indian decision-makers had overlooked this possibility. If the Chinese occupied the passes they would have had the tactical upper hand in any future conflict as they would have control over dominating military heights and be able to look right into Sikkim.

In the days following the meeting of the senior military

commanders where it was decided that India would not engage the Chinese at the border but withdraw to inland defensive positions, Sagat decided to visit every part of the area under his command. He spent considerable time on ground trying to understand the lay of the land better. He interacted with battalion and company commanders in the area and spoke with local post commanders and soldiers at forward posts.

In the Sino-Indian war of 1962, some senior military leaders ignored the feedback from ground commanders that left them bereft of a realistic understanding of the evolving Chinese attack. This led to disastrous decisions. In 1965, by the time Chinese forces arrived at the doorstep of Sikkim in September, Sagat had gained enough understanding of the terrain to take a bold decision. He had also grown confident about the ability of his division to repulse a Chinese attack.

Expectedly, Major General Harcharan Singh, the commander of 27 Division, responsible for Jelep La, acted in accordance with the directives from the 33 Corps headquarters in Siliguri and retreated. The forward post on the Jelep La pass, which was situated on the watershed line, was thus vacated by the Indian army.

Sagat, on the other hand, disagreed with his superior commanders and argued that if India were to vacate the Nathu La pass and retreat behind the watershed, the

Chinese would be well placed to occupy the pass and simply control the watershed.[19] This would give them a decisive advantage of dominating the lower region of Gangtok and the entire state of Sikkim. It also had another ramification: an advancing Chinese army could then cut off the one narrow strip of land that connected India's northeast to its mainland. This narrow strip, located south of Sikkim and part of West Bengal, is called the Siliguri Corridor,[20] as well as the chicken's neck, alluding to its vulnerability. At its slimmest, the corridor is 25 kilometres wide and also connects the Indian mainland to Bhutan and Bangladesh (then East Pakistan) by road.

For the Chinese, the Siliguri Corridor could thus serve as the 'anvil' for a hammer blow to shatter Indian defences in the northeast.[21] There was also the fear that PLA forces could advance, scythe through the narrow chicken's neck and link up with Pakistani forces in East Pakistan. (Till 1971, Pakistani armed forces occupied the land to the east of the Siliguri Corridor, thus enhancing the corridor's vulnerability.) Given this background the decision of the corps headquarters to withdraw from Nathu La was baffling. Sagat remained steadfastly defiant and refused to evict his troops from the forward post at Nathu La. He believed that regardless of any provocation by the Chinese, not an inch of ground was to be surrendered.[22]

From the increased presence of troops on the Chinese side, it appeared that their plan may have been twofold: one, to make India commit its troops on two fronts, and two, to push India down the watershed and occupy the heights.

Sagat was known to take decisions that often irked his seniors. Earlier, before moving to Sikkim, he was posted at the 15 Corps headquarters in Kashmir, where his relations with his boss, Lieutenant General J.S. Dhillon, were often tetchy.

As soon as India decided to withdraw from Jelep La, China promptly seized the vacated pass.[23] The Indian army would later return to occupy the three vacant peaks flanking it – Sher, Cub and Cheetah – and therefore dominate the Chinese troops that now sat at the lower height of the Jelep La pass. Tactically, the Indians still had an advantage – dominating the enemy by occupying the higher ground in the area. The psychological advantage, however, had been wrested by the PLA. The Chinese had managed to harry and evict the Indian army from Jelep La without firing a bullet! The decision on Nathu La thus became an even more critical one – both from a point of view of strategy as well as the morale of the troops.

Sagat refused to withdraw his troops from Nathu La even if it caused his relationship with Lieutenant General G.G. Bewoor to turn prickly. He stressed that as a division commander he was authorized to take a call pertaining to a forward post in his jurisdiction. Finally, everyone reluctantly came around to his proposition.

The Indian decision to hold Nathu La, especially after the quick withdrawal from Jelep La, left the Chinese dumbfounded. It also appeared strange that in the same corps zone, one forward post had been vacated while the other was still occupied. This irked the Chinese, who increased the frequency of firing exchanges along the sector, much to the concern of the Indian side.

One evening when heavy firing lit up the hills, Bewoor was terribly concerned that a conflict might break out and indecision got the better of him. Would holding the forward lines at Nathu La goad China to attack India? Anticipating that tensions in the headquarters could possibly result in a reversal of his decision, Sagat walked out of office to avoid confronting Bewoor on the phone.

As expected, an anxious Bewoor called up the division headquarters that evening. Lieutenant Colonel Lakhpat Singh, Sagat's staff officer, had to bear the brunt of the corps commander's fury when he informed him that Sagat was not in office.

Meanwhile, opposite the Nathu La pass on the Tibetan side, the Chinese had assembled loudspeakers – twenty-one of them! They blared all day, rebuking the Indians for their actions, screaming that destiny had a rerun of 1962 in store for them. They reminded the Indians about the might of the Chinese army. The slogans, which oscillated between homilies about the virtues of communism that benefited the poor soldier and rubbishing the Indian soldiers, were in Hindi. However, they had been translated into 'shudh' Hindi. Meant to be menacing and threatening, they ended up being incomprehensible to the Indian troops who were used to more colloquial language.

The onset of winter following the India–Pakistan ceasefire of late September 1965 rendered movement in the high altitudes cumbersome and challenging. China, however, persevered with a low-scale war of attrition via a series of attempts to dominate the border. Four skirmishes were reported between late September and December. Mortars were used to relentlessly pummel locations on the Indian side accompanied with a continued barrage of small-arms fire, periodically raising alarm bells in the Indian military headquarters.

In December 1965 when a patrol of Assam Rifles was attacked by Chinese troops at around 18,000 feet on the Giagong plateau in north Sikkim and the patrolling Indian soldiers were killed, Sagat travelled to the site of the action. The troops, not used to generals arriving at the front, were genuinely surprised. Sagat even walked all the way to the base when he was refused a helicopter

Major General Randhir Sinh (retd)

Sagat Singh (second from left) with officers
and troops at Nathu La.

by the Eastern Air Command for his return.[24]

The skirmishes and deadlock along the border
continued. The extent of China's desire to occupy the
Nathu La watershed would be revealed in the next couple
of years. During the events of 1965 in Sikkim, China was
simply preparing for the long haul.

~

General Sagat, by refusing to withdraw from Nathu
La, had called China's bluff. Taken aback by the Indian
decision to stay put in Nathu La, the Chinese decided
to wait for the right opportunity to reopen the Sikkim

chapter.

The crisis game had predicted China's attack on India on the Sikkim border. The participants discussed the subsequent warm reception the PLA would receive from locals in Gangtok. The analysis was based on Sikkim's growing discontentment with the Indian government. Since India's independence, the Sikkim royals had been uncomfortable about the role the Indian government played in their state. Now the war of 1965 and the arrival of Hope Cooke, the new queen of Sikkim, had thrown the relationship between India and Sikkim into a flux, and China was waiting to exploit the weaknesses.

In 1964, Palden Thondup, the Chogyal, had married Hope Cooke in a glamorous royal wedding in the

Palden Thondup and Hope Cooke.

Himalayas. The western world was enamoured by the fairy-tale romance between Hope, a young all-American girl from Brooklyn, and the royal from Sikkim. Their wedding had all the ingredients of a Hollywood romance. Hope was compared to Grace Kelly, the film actress who had married the king of Monaco.[25] The wedding was a high-profile event that drew ambassadors from nine nations, including the newly appointed US ambassador to India, John Kenneth Galbraith. The list of dignitaries was long and included Indian leaders, bureaucrats and key socialites of Sikkim. Indira Gandhi was one of the attendees. Hope Cooke had put the obscure, tiny Buddhist kingdom on the world map. But Hope would also cause the unsettling of India–Sikkim relations, perhaps instigated in no small measure by China.

In 1962, when China and India were at war, Hope, whom Palden Thondup was then courting, had written a cheque to the Indian Prime Minister's Defence Fund. The war of 1962 was an outcome of differences between India and China over the boundary they shared, which excluded the border involving Sikkim. At that time, the war completely bypassed Sikkim since China was also consciously cultivating support amongst the Sikkim royals. India did not take kindly to China's interactions with the royals. An increasingly aggressive and expansionist China, which had taken over Tibet, was suspected to have its sight on Sikkim and there were concerns that a military thrust could follow a brief diplomatic parry. When Tashi Namgyal, Palden's reclusive father, passed away in December 1963, an official note of condolence arrived for Palden Thondup from Peking. Similarly, when Palden was crowned as the king in 1965, Zhou Enlai was among the first leaders to congratulate him. On both occasions, India did not take to the gestures kindly.

In 1965, the stand-off between the Chinese and Indians at the Sikkim–Tibet border had ironically resulted in increasing tensions between India and Sikkim. As India's protectorate, Sikkim's defence was in Delhi's hands. But Delhi's statement saying that it would not allow China to violate 'India's border' had bothered the Chogyal. On the advice of Nari Rustomji, the Indian political officer and his dewan, the king issued a statement reiterating Sikkim's independent identity in the dispute between India and China.

Hope did not believe in shrouding her opinions in diplomatic tact and publicly aired her disenchantment about the treatment Sikkim got from the Indian government. She felt India's statement was typical of the arrogance that India had shown towards Sikkim until then.

The princess attracted ire from the Indian establishment as she rapidly grew into an advocate of greater autonomy for Sikkim. While China and India traded accusations, Hope Cooke and her sister-in-law, Coocoola, decided to vent to the media in the UK. While the two women had their personal differences, they bonded over their dislike for India and the way it had undermined Sikkim's identity during the 1965 war.

Coocoola would tell Hope, 'They [Indians] are calling Sikkim an area of India and talking about the border as the India–China border. The nerve. We've got to stop this. We've got to remind people of Sikkim's identity before it gets lost.'[26] But unable to garner support for her cause in London, Hope returned to Sikkim disillusioned. Politics and war weren't the only things getting her down. Her life in the kingdom was unhappy and friendless. Her marriage was a strained mess as a result of her husband's philandering ways which left Hope depressed and lonely.

As the distance between the Gyalmo and the Chogyal widened, the one person in Gangtok who was a bright spot for Hope was their friend Sagat Singh.

The royal couple had grown close to the general since he was posted in the kingdom and would meet him often in the evenings. Hope found solace in Sagat's company and occasionally found herself flirting with him.[27] Interestingly, though Hope and Sagat shared vastly divergent views on the India–China–Sikkim situation, the friendship between the general and the royals continued

Sagat Singh with the royal couple at their palace
in Gangtok, circa 1965.

to grow despite the stand-off with China at the Sikkim
border during the 1965 war. Hope and Sagat had
divergent views on the India–China–Sikkim situation.
Hope believed that the Indian government overplayed
the Chinese threat, using it as a pretext to deny Sikkim its
political freedom and true identity. Sagat, who headed the
Indian state's military forces deployed in Sikkim, felt that
the Chinese presence across the border was an imminent
threat to Sikkim and the surrounding Indian territory,
which needed to be countered militarily. Their differing
perceptions, however, did not affect their friendship.

Hope found the general to be wickedly charming. Sagat's phone calls announcing his return to Gangtok from the field posts were a 'source of happiness' for her. 'Our general', as she referred to him, was always around to help the couple. Once, when in Delhi, Hope received a desperate call from the Chogyal. Their son Palden was terribly ill. Within an hour, the general helped arrange a plane for Hope from Delhi to Siliguri, from where the Chogyal's car took her to Gangtok. When Hope finally arrived at the palace, the general was around with the Chogyal. Sagat remained a family friend: a military mate to Chogyal and a close companion to Hope.[28] Sagat would invite her to the parties held by the local infantry battalions[29] and the two would often spend quite a bit of time together.

The Chogyal was an honorary major general of 8 Gorkha Rifles, the regiment to which Sagat belonged, and had always felt at home with his officer mates from the Indian army such as Sagat and his senior, General Sam Manekshaw, who commanded the Eastern Command of the army. Interestingly, one day during the war, while his wife was expressing her unequivocal disapproval of the Indian government, the Chogyal, attired in his Indian army uniform, with the emblem of crossed Gorkha khukris pinned on the epaulettes on his shoulders, decided to appear for a media interview. 'One's really not quite sure what they [China] want to do . . . I don't think they meant an all-out war, so one assumes it was really to tie down Indian troops in this part of the world from maybe going across to the Pakistani side.'[30]

The bonhomie that the royal couple shared with the military in Sikkim was in stark contrast to the bitterness with the civil administration. One of the reasons for the disenchantment of the royal couple with the Indian government – and the opening this created for China – was the lack of chemistry between the couple and the appointed civil services administrators sent to Sikkim. On the other hand, Hope and Thondup's relations with the army in Sikkim remained those of mutual respect. Hope later wrote in her autobiography that the Indian army was largely respectful towards the people of Sikkim, which endeared the locals towards them.[31]

While the royals continued to raise the question of Sikkim's identity, a domestic problem had begun to surface. The British had always viewed Tibet as a strategic buffer between the Sikkimese kingdom and China and thus chose to build roads to the Tibetan capital of Lhasa to facilitate trade and business. To build infrastructure, they required a large number of labourers. In the early 1900s, the British encouraged the migration of Nepalis into Sikkim as workers. In time, migrant Nepalis, which included workers who had settled in Sikkim, grew to become a substantial majority in the state, outnumbering

Sagat (third from left) and Palden Thondup (fourth from left) shared a warm camaraderie. Palden was an honorary Indian army officer.

the indigenous Lepchas and Bhutias.[32]

Despite the demographic inversion, the Chogyals implemented archaic tax laws where impoverished immigrant labourers, who mostly worked on farms and villages and were desperately poor, paid higher taxes than other Sikkimese. The poorly paid labourers increasingly began to view the Indian state as a source of support. This vocal set of the population would play an important role in the assimilation of Sikkim into India a decade later.

The Chogyal was unwilling to embrace democracy which he believed would benefit the sizeable Nepali community over the Lepchas and Bhutias. The discontent brewing amongst the Nepalis had caught the interest of a local politician named Lhendup Dorjee who took up their cause and organized a people's movement against the monarchy. Popularly known as Kazi, Dorjee had the covert support of the Indian government and had begun to unsettle the monarchy. Hope's outburst against India at this time could also have been a result of the worries that the local movement was causing the monarchy. This was the context of China's intentions regarding Sikkim and the dispute over the Sikkim–Tibet border.

As the exchanges and skirmishes between India and China continued in Sikkim, the two original warring sides, India and Pakistan, were edging their way towards reluctant peace at Tashkent. As mentioned earlier, a ceasefire had been declared on 22 September 1965.

On 3 January 1966, Ayub Khan and Lal Bahadur Shastri flew to Tashkent and spent over a week in negotiations. Though the Pakistani army had done well initially, India had ended the war with an advantage, having almost progressed all the way to Lahore and Sialkot. The Pakistani government had ventured into the talks after its state media had publicized to its people how the Pakistani army had won the war. The Pakistan government now couldn't appear to have lost a war that they had started. On 7 January 1966, Ayub and Bhutto tried to bring up the issue of Kashmir, which Shastri refused to discuss.[33] A difference of opinion was also developing between the two Pakistani leaders, with Bhutto being obstructionist and Ayub more conciliatory. Ayub was left with two options: either walk away from the summit and be damned by the international community, or sign the agreement without any gains on Kashmir and risk a hostile reaction at home. Time was running out for the president.

To be fair, Ayub had come a long way from his initial bluster before the war. But he still needed to save face. And so on 7 January the tall, strapping Pathan summoned every ounce of his soldierly courage to plead with the pint-sized Indian prime minister, '*Kashmir ke maamle mein kuchh aisa kar deejiye ki main apne mulk mein munh dikhaney ke kaabil rahoon.*' (Please help me on the issue of Kashmir so that I can face my people back home.) The canny Indian prime minister smiled and politely declined.

The negotiations divided the Pakistani camp into the hawks of Bhutto and the doves of Ayub. Seeing this rift, Shastri increased the pressure on them, setting a tight timeline for the talks to be concluded. Come what may he planned to head home on 11 January. As if on cue, on 8 January, a fresh complaint came from China about aggressive Indian attitude. The new Chinese threat to strike back, bombastic and menacing in expression, had started to sound farcical, as there was no specific mention in the Chinese note of what exactly they disapproved of in India's actions at Tashkent or otherwise.

As the impasse was becoming difficult to break, Alexei Kosygin, the Soviet premier moderating the talks, decided to try something different. The day after the Chinese threat was made, he offered to take Ayub out for a day to clear his head. Kosygin's talk with Ayub clearly had an effect: on 10 January, a peace treaty, in which India made no concessions on Kashmir, was signed between the two nations. However, the Tashkent treaty wasn't about to end without drama. Shastri had agreed to pre-war positions at Tashkent, which meant keeping the Kashmir Valley with India – a position that political parties in India didn't agree with since they wanted the entire state (including Pakistan-occupied Kashmir) as part of the deal. Both sides made some territorial gains at Tashkent but what riled many in Delhi was that India handed back important strategic positions such as the town of Tithwal and the Haji Pir pass.[34]

Hours after signing the treaty, and the night before Shastri was set to return to India via Kabul on 11 January, he suffered a heart attack. Veteran journalist Kuldeep Nayyar, who was on that tour with the prime minister, recalled, 'The assistants were packing the luggage at 1.20 a.m., when they saw Shastri at the door. With great difficulty Shastri asked: "Where is doctor sahib?" It was in the sitting room that a racking cough convulsed

Shastri, and his personal assistants helped him to bed. His assistant Jagan Nath gave him water and remarked: "Babuji, now you will be all right." Shastri only touched his chest and then became unconscious.' He never woke up again.

The irony of what transpired in Tashkent couldn't have been more poignant. Ayub Khan, the bete noire against whose country India had just fought a bitter war, became the head pall bearer carrying Shastri's coffin to the Russian aircraft waiting to carry him to Delhi.[35] His sudden death sent shock waves through the country. Indian delegates thus returned home with a treaty resolution that they wanted. But they also brought home India's hero of the 1965 war in a coffin. The political-military equation between the politicians and the military in India had changed during his time, almost compensating for the disaster of the 1962 war, which was an outcome of the military generals being left in the cold and not taken into consideration in important strategic matters by then defence minister, Krishna Menon. The freedom given by Shastri to his generals to seize the moment and expand the war outside Kashmir had been unprecedented. As prime minister he took the war to the enemy camp and a truce was called when the Indian army was in Sialkot and was staring at the city of Lahore a few miles away. Many would question his decision to agree to the truce despite having the upper hand. However, Shastri, in a short tenure, had managed to restore the pride of the nation and its military after the debacle of 1962. The turnaround had begun.

~

Four important outcomes emerged from the war of 1965 that would define the course of the subcontinent's history. One, the war and the Tashkent treaty deepened the growing rift between Pakistan's army-backed president and a civilian leader.[36] The result of the war and Pakistan's lack of cohesion at Tashkent marked Ayub's fall and Bhutto's rise in Pakistani politics.

Two, as the US stayed out of the conflict, the Soviets steered the difficult agreement between neighbours which the West was happy to watch from a distance. The Soviets would strengthen their presence in South Asia, especially their relationship with India.[37] But this alliance would further antagonize another stakeholder – China.

The third outcome was the ascent of China as an influencer of ample guile and patience, which was now seeking to use surrogate means to extend its domination in the region. From here on, China would lend weight as a third dimension in the region to the existing bipolar power balance between the US and USSR. Through the threats and ultimatums during the war, China demonstrated its ability to sway India's decisions on committing troops on a second front. By unambiguously encouraging Pakistan in the war against India and by reinforcing India's fears of a two-front war,[38] China forced the world to take seriously the presence of the dragon in the region.

The fourth outcome was an underrated one, but perhaps the most heartwarming for India. India had, for the first time, launched an attack to counter an opponent and made several inroads into Pakistan. China, the more testing adversary, had sensed an opening in the east. It decided to test India's resolve in Sikkim and expected to find the muddle-headedness that typified India's political approach and a lack of courage that characterized its military leadership in its bungling defeat in 1962. Instead, the pushback at Nathu La, where a defiant Sagat Singh refused to budge, would prove to be a monumental example of far-sighted decision-making. The events that followed would validate his decision to hold the pass, which had gone unnoticed amidst the war.

Part 2

The Battles of Nathu La
and Cho La

4

China's Psychological Tactics: Softening Up the Enemy Before the Storm

China had used the India–Pakistan war of 1965 to extend its growing influence in the Sikkim region. Chairman of the Communist Party of China, Mao Zedong's strategy was to put more pressure on India. Mao wanted to tie India down in multiple arenas and make Delhi fight fires on many fronts so that China's creeping into Sikkim would get a distracted, feeble response from an exhausted New Delhi. Indeed, the 1960s were a period when China instigated much trouble in India: there were insurgencies, first in Mizoram and then in Nagaland and West Bengal, all funded by China. There were constant skirmishes on the Sikkim–Tibet border and tension between the Indian government and the Sikkimese monarchy. There was uneasiness on the Doklam plateau.

These disparate events may seem unrelated, but the Chinese hand is the common thread that runs through them all. Mao himself needed desperately to distract his Chinese subjects from the terror that the cultural revolution had unleashed in the country. In China at that time a paranoid Mao was busy purging party leaders he viewed as threats. In this period, a deeply suspicious Mao formed an inner circle comprising his wife Jiang Qing, minister Lin Bao and chief of intelligence Kang Sheng to identify and purge dissidents and rivals. Deng Xiaoping, who was once a part of the circle of leaders, was targeted and Deng's proclivity towards market-friendly measures resulted in his incarceration. He was sent to work as an ordinary factory worker and his son, Deng Pufang, was tortured, and thrown out of the window of a three-storey building. Pufang survived but was disabled for life.

Kang Sheng, who was given the mandate to carry out Mao's orders, unleashed a reign of devastating brutality during this period. A number of people disappeared. Those who had fallen out of favour were paraded through the streets of China's cities, with dunce caps on their heads and humiliating placards around their necks. With so much upheaval and internal turmoil, Mao needed to rally people behind him and there was no easier way to do so than by stirring up nationalist emotions. India was the perfect sacrificial lamb. In this chapter we go on a brief tour of the fires lit by the Chinese which the Indian government was fighting.

~

Lal Bahadur Shastri's death in Tashkent after the 1965 war left a void that was filled by Indira Gandhi. Adopting a fierce posture in the face of hostility came naturally to her, which meant that she was ruthless in launching pre-emptive strikes against her enemies, external and internal.

A month and four days into assuming the office of India's prime minister in 1966, Indira Gandhi had to deal with an outbreak of a rebellion in the north-eastern state of Mizoram. The rebels were trained by the Pakistani army in camps inside East Pakistan (now Bangladesh), and later sustained by China, which supplied wireless transmitters, medicines and funds through the Chinese consulate in Dhaka.[1] A few years later, the Chinese support would become more explicit, with Mizo rebels crossing over into China to train under the PLA.

On 28 February 1966, insurgents from the Mizo National Army (MNA) revolted against the Indian state, attacking Border Security Force and Assam Rifles garrisons in the districts of Lunglei and Champhai. By

2 March, fierce fighting had erupted in the state and the MNA guerrillas had overrun the Aizawl treasury and armoury. It was threatening to capture more ground and humiliate the Indian authorities. The Indian state had to respond soon but Indira Gandhi's decision was not merely swift and harsh, it was unprecedented and brutal.

On 5 March, at about 11.30 a.m., four fighter jets of the Indian Air Force – French-built Dassault Ouragan fighters or Toofanis, as they were called, and British Hunters – took off from Tezpur, Kumbigram and Jorhat in Assam. Two caribou planes with bombs would be flown by two young pilots, Rajesh Pilot and Suresh Kalmadi, who went on to become well-known politicians in the latter part of their lives. The jets took Aizawl by surprise, bombing the town. The next day, the bombings intensified, causing casualties and spreading fear. By the time the planes retreated to their bases, Aizawl was a mess. Four of the largest areas of the city – Republic Veng, Hmeichche Veng, Dawrpui Veng and Chhinga Veng – had been razed to the ground. Indira Gandhi didn't hesitate to drop bombs on her own people to kill the Mizo insurgents. That was the first and, hopefully, the last time India would ever bomb its own people.

The bombing of Aizawl is a blot on our history and Mizoram observed a black day each year for fifty years on the anniversary of the bombing. As expressed by the sources interviewed, the incident revealed the new prime minister's unambiguous preference for using force early on over dialogue to quell enemies. She had shown a ready instinct for using the military as a core instrument of resolving a crisis. In the process, she had begun to develop a much firmer, long-lasting relationship with the Indian army than her father or his ministers ever did. But while one challenge had been overcome, at least for the moment, a steady stream of others lay ahead.

In early 1967, Mao got an opportunity to fan a crisis in the lowlands of north Bengal, not too far from the location of Sagat Singh's 17 Division in the neighbouring state of Sikkim. For centuries, agricultural land in the region had been largely owned by landlords, or jotedars, some of whom brutally exploited the peasants. Landowners would refuse to pay the peasants their dues, usurp land and belongings, harass women and children and drive ryots out of their homes. In 1967 a peasants' council in Siliguri, north Bengal, declared its intent to enforce the redistribution of land. There was a simmering anger underneath the feudal surface. The epicentre of the labour uprising taking shape was a small village called Naxalbari, about 40 kilometres from Siliguri in the chicken's neck that connected the larger part of India to its north-eastern part, which was also India's Achilles heel in case of an attack by China to cut India off from its north-eastern states, as explained in the previous chapters.

In May 1967 Bigul Kisan, a sharecropper,[2] went to ask his landowner for payment of dues and was beaten up. In response a group of people rounded up the landowner and his men and lynched them with arrows, stones and spears. A few days later, Sonam Wangdi, the inspector of a police station, received an urgent complaint from a village called Jharugaon about some people who had been involved in forcible harvesting. He gathered a few policemen and rushed to the village where the local workers surrounded them. He was faced with an angry crowd that attacked the police. They showered arrows on the cops and within moments, Wangdi lay dead. His men, fearing for their lives, ran away.

Each day more such incidents would take place, marking the beginning of a violent communist movement in Bengal. Thousands of villagers armed with bows, arrows and spears rebelled against landowners and took over their lands and granaries. By the end of May 1967 the movement had blown into an armed uprising[3] that had taken its name from the village where it started – Naxalbari. The insurrection was led by fiery leaders such as Charu Mazumdar, Kanu Sanyal and Jangal Santhal who dreamt of a Maoist revolution of peasants and workers far beyond this one district. In urban Calcutta, the movement fired up an entire generation, as an anonymous poet wrote on the walls of Calcutta: 'Amar bari, tomar bari / Naxalbari Naxalbari' (My home, Naxalbari / Your home, Naxalbari). The uprising challenged the validity of the state.[4]

On 5 July 1967, the *People's Daily*, China's official newspaper, carried a gleeful editorial about India's internal challenges titled 'Spring Thunder Over India'. It read: 'A peal of spring thunder has crashed over the land of India. Revolutionary peasants in Darjeeling area have risen in rebellion. Under the leadership of a revolutionary group of the Indian communist party, a red area of revolutionary armed struggle has been established in India.'[5]

A left-wing peasant revolution in a border state close to the Siliguri Corridor was just the kind of schism that China looked to exploit.

Predictably, Charu Mazumdar and his comrades were soon invited by Mao to China. Mazumdar and his colleagues Khokhon Mazumdar, Khudan Malick, Deepak Biswas and Kanu Sanyal soon set off on an arduous trek that took them through the forests of the northeast and the swamps of Myanmar to meet Mao, accompanied by a Mandarin-speaking guide sent by the Chinese embassy in Kathmandu who helped the four Maoists across Myanmar and Tibet.

When the chairman finally appeared before the Naxal leaders, they were enthralled. Mazumdar even coined a phrase: 'Chiner Chairman, Amader Chairman' (China's chairman is our chairman). The comrades were given training in handling machine guns and automated rifles, lobbing grenades and planting anti-personnel mines.[6]

The Naxal and the Mizo were not the only insurgencies that Mao supported. The Chinese had identified India's northeast as an area where they could create a lot more trouble. In fact the Nagas were the first anti-government force in India to receive support from China.[7] Mao even encouraged a radical branch within the Communist Party of India to forsake the parliamentary path and take to the rebel road instead, which later resulted in a breakaway faction known as the Communist Party of India (Marxist–Leninist).[8] The other outcome of Chinese mischief was India's determination to nip in the bud the desire of autonomy of Himalayan border states.[9] This resolve was tested most strongly in Sikkim, where the Chinese were fishing in the waters of a troubled relationship.

As soon as Indira Gandhi assumed office in 1966, a long-standing desire of the associate kingdom-state of Sikkim was on the king's mind. Palden Thondup had known Indira Gandhi for a long time and she even attended his wedding. He sought a change in the treaty Sikkim had signed with India in 1950. On the one hand, he enjoyed a cordial relationship with the Indian army, but on the other, he was sceptical about the growing powers of bureaucrats who had been posted as political officers in Sikkim. He had been asking for changes in the treaty which would give greater powers to the kingdom. Palden and Indira Gandhi were cordial, but he was aware of the iron fist of the new Indian prime minister. Moreover, since any change was unlikely before the ensuing elections in early 1967, he waited for the right moment to broach the treaty change with her. But in the summer of 1966, as Palden was biding his time, his wife, Hope Cooke, seen by many parliamentarians in India as a CIA agent – an assumption not based on any evidence – jumped the gun, fatally wounding their project of Sikkimese autonomy. Hope Cooke, disillusioned with the indifference with which her protests against India had been treated during the war of 1965, wrote an article in the *Bulletin of the Institute of Tibetology* in Gangtok. Titled 'Sikkimese Theory of Landholding and the Darjeeling Grant', the article questioned the legitimacy of the grant of Darjeeling district to British India in 1835.[10] She argued that Darjeeling was wrongly given to the British in the past by Sikkim and that it should now be returned to its rightful owner, the Sikkimese monarchy. In 1835 the Chogyal of Sikkim had gifted Darjeeling to British India on the understanding that a certain amount would be paid as annual subsidy to Sikkim.[11] Hope Cooke's article couldn't have been more ill-timed. Indira Gandhi's political future was unsure. She faced stiff competition from rivals within her own party as she headed into the elections of 1967.[12] A headwind of anger and serious internal issues greeted her elevation as a leader. Despite edging out the older Morarji Desai through a secret ballot in internal party elections, Indira was ridiculed by more formidable and older parliamentarians for her inexperience. The economy had plummeted: a trade deficit of Rs 930 crore had sent the economy spiralling into crisis after the United States suspended aid to both India and Pakistan after the 1965 war. To make matters worse, the country was wracked by drought and food shortage after the rains had failed for two successive years.[13] Indira Gandhi couldn't afford another crisis. Given that Hope Cooke was seen as an American agent by several newspapers and MPs in India, Indira Gandhi rushed to prove her credentials as an anti-imperialist leader. Under no circumstances would she entertain the Sikkimese monarchy's pleas of renegotiating the treaty, especially not with China waiting to pounce.

But while the political wrangles and the issue over Hope Cooke exercised much of the media, the skirmishes along the border of Sikkim were going unnoticed. China's aim was to keep up the pressure on Indian soldiers with occasional attacks along the border. There were a few incidents when Indian patrols and soldiers were even fired upon. Though Chinese aggression would be met with resistance, there was no aggression from India. Some of the border spats were patently ridiculous. Once, a group of Indian paratroopers, after an argument with the Chinese, decided to vent their anger by shedding their clothes and dancing naked before them.[14] The Chinese of course complained to the Indian defence ministry and the incident was laughed off.

But Sikkim wasn't India's only protectorate where the Chinese were instigating trouble. In 1966, another incident occurred in Sikkim's backyard involving the most prized piece of real estate in the region called Doklam or Zhoglam (in the Tibetan language), or Donglang in the Chinese language – a plateau that lay to the east of Sikkim in Bhutan, an Indian protectorate. Doklam is just south of the Chumbi valley which itself juts into the Siliguri Corridor in India. A Chinese presence in Doklam could help them control the crucial Jampheri ridge that overlooks the Siliguri Corridor.

In October 1966, when Chinese soldiers entered the Doklam plateau in Bhutan, India strongly disapproved of the move and responded immediately, leading to furious diplomatic exchanges between India and China.[15] The Chinese government accused India of concocting 'stories about "intrusions" into Bhutanese territory by Chinese herdsmen and patrols'.[16] China wanted to test whether India would take up the cudgels on behalf of its protectorate. Chinese actions may also have been a ploy to test Bhutan's faith in India's capability to defend its interests.

Indira Gandhi didn't take long to lash out at a press conference, asserting strongly that India was committed to protecting Bhutan. She maintained that since Bhutan was India's protectorate state, the security of Bhutan was India's responsibility. China protested immediately. The official news agency Hsinhua (now Xinhua) shot back, calling India's moves despicable and charged India with interference in Bhutan's affairs under the guise of protection.

But the insurgencies and the volatile Sikkim–Bhutan–Tibet borders weren't the only sites of Chinese aggression. In a bid to whip up nationalist sentiments Mao was going after Indians inside China. In 1967, reports from the Indian consul revealed that a Sikh gurdwara in Tientsin (now Tianjin) had been desecrated and a Parsi temple in Shanghai had been occupied by the Red Army.[17]

In another reported incident, an argument that broke out between an Indian dairy owner and his Chinese employee ended in the two coming to blows. The local newspapers spared no effort in featuring this incident which drew the ire of local labour unions that forced the dairy owners to give in to their employees' demands. Most Indians who lived in Shanghai were dairy owners and were badly affected.

The Chinese authorities also started a headcount of Indian citizens. The census search found that twenty-four Indian citizens were in China and most of them were of mixed parentage.[18] The Chinese claimed the rest of the Indians in that country to be citizens under their law and the Indian government duly withdrew their Indian passports to save them from persecution.

China was also increasing the gap of military capability between itself and India. In 1964 China had conducted nuclear tests sending shock waves in India. On 27 October 1966, when a Dong Feng-2 medium range ballistic missile with a 12 kiloton nuclear warhead flew dangerously over human-inhabited areas before successfully striking its target in Lop Nur in the desserts of Xinjiang, it was evident this was China's way of announcing its intentions to the world.[19] A year after exerting a significant influence over India in the 1965 Indo-Pak war, China flew a nuclear missile, which was an ominous sign of things to come for an India that had no nuclear capability. China had already conducted its first nuclear test in 1964, a year before the war and, on 17 June 1967, it would test its first thermonuclear device, conducting more nuclear tests in a shorter time span than any of the other nuclear powers.

These seemingly small, unconnected events – the Naga and Mizo rebellions, the Naxal uprising, the Sikkimese monarchy's attempted revolt, the stand-off at Doklam – signalled the deep-seated insecurity that China harboured and were all portents of the battles of Cho La and Nathu La that were around the corner.

5

1966–67: Warriors Arrive at the Watershed

Throughout 1965 and 1966 the relationship between India and China – on the Sikkim border in particular but also otherwise – remained tense. In this chapter we meet the characters who played the leading roles in the 1967 battles of Cho La and Nathu La.

The Gorkhas of Nepal were an elite fighting force during the British period who served valiantly in several wars in India and across the world. At the time of India's independence in 1947,[1] some Gorkha soldiers slated to be absorbed by the British army opted to stay back and serve in a newly formed Indian army. Thus, 11 Gorkha Rifles was born in 1948 as one of India's newest infantry regiments.[2]

The Indian army is organized into several commands. Currently there are six operational commands and one training command. Each command is led by a senior lieutenant general and comprises military formations known as corps. Under each corps, there are a number of divisions (usually three to four). A division comprises several fighting and support elements, which could be from the infantry, artillery, signals, engineers etc. (like 17 Mountain Division in Sikkim did). Under each division are a few brigades. Each brigade, in turn, comprises a few units known as battalions.

The battalion comprises companies, each made up of three platoons. A platoon has three sections, which are the smallest units in the army organization structure (for more details refer to Appendix 1).

In 1964, Kul Bhushan Joshi (KB) of the 5th Battalion of 11 Gorkha Rifles (commonly referred to as 5/11 Gorkha Rifles or 5/11 GR)[3] came to Sikkim and established the Cho La post at the border, according to the sources interviewed for this book.

Three years later, he would lead an energetic but inexperienced bunch of Gorkha soldiers in the battle of Cho La as commanding officer of the 7th Battalion of the 11 Gorkha Regiment. Alongside the 11 Gorkha Regiment in Sikkim were the Grenadiers,[4] amongst the most illustrious and experienced regiments of the Indian army. The Grenadiers' 2nd Battalion commanded by Rai Singh would arrive in Sikkim in 1967 and later move to the border at Nathu La. All the brigades in the Sikkim sector came under the leadership of Sagat who was the division commander of 17 Infantry Division based in Gangtok.[5]

~

Commissioned in 1950 as a second lieutenant into the 5th Battalion of 11 Gorkha Rifles, Kul Bhushan Joshi accompanied the battalion in 1964 to Sikkim. KB – who had grown up in Burma at the time when Japanese planes fighting the British and their allies were bombing that country during the Second World War – was tasked with establishing a forward post at the Sikkim–China border, where weather conditions were expectedly harsh and roads nonexistent. In 1964, the forward post he established borrowed its name from the pass on which it stood. It would be called Cho La. Lacking adequate warm clothing, boots and digging implements, KB and his men almost perished in the freezing winds and blizzards, while doggedly building bunkers and trenches among the rocks to prepare for the eventuality of a battle. At that time, however, there were no PLA troops on the Chinese side and hence the perception of threat was lower. After this posting KB and his battalion were moved elsewhere.

Little did KB know that a few years later, in 1967, he would return to Cho La to fight a battle that would change history forever.

In 1967, KB was appointed second in command of the 7th Battalion of 11 Gorkha Rifles, stationed at Cho La. The battalion was raised in Dehradun in the wake of the 1965 war. He found, to his surprise, that there were seventeen subalterns (consisting of lieutenants and second lieutenants, with the latter being the entry level rank of a commissioned officer in the army at that time) in the battalion – an unusually high number. It began to be called the subaltern battalion and was sometimes mockingly referred to as the kancha paltan (a battalion of young tyros).

The new battalion was untested and it was the first field posting for many of the boys. A hard taskmaster, the colonel who headed the 7th Battalion prepared his soldiers for imminent battle. He put them through rigorous drills, honing the battle skills of his hardy Gorkha troops who, having grown up in the hills of Nepal and Darjeeling, already had the advantage of stamina. But destiny had in store a twist in the script for KB. Upright but obdurate, the colonel hadn't been on the best of terms with his boss, the brigade commander. Furious at his battalion being given poor stores and equipment, the impulsive colonel hollered to his commander: 'I am not commanding a labour army,' and abruptly quit the army to settle in his farm in the hills of Himachal.[6]

One day before leaving he called the officers and told them, 'Keep your khukris sharpened for the Chinese. If the Chinese ever try to break through Cho La, they would be khukried by the Gorkhas.' He had sensed the dark portents ahead. Next in the chain of command, KB found himself at the helm of the 7th Battalion of 11 Gorkha Rifles as its new commanding officer.

The situation in Sikkim along the border with China had grown thorny in the past two years. As mentioned in Part 1, in 1965, the Indian army had chosen to occupy and not withdraw from Nathu La. There were serious concerns that the intermittent firing between India and China that characterized the Sikkim–Tibet border could turn into a larger military confrontation. No one wanted a war. But who could predict the reactions of hostile men in an isolated high-altitude zone where a lack of oxygen could turn a soldier dizzy enough to pull the trigger of a loaded weapon, despite years of training to control their impulses.

In 1964 when KB had set up the Cho La post, the land around it was mostly unoccupied. Now, in 1967, however, barely a few metres separated the Indians from the bristling Chinese army.

KB was catapulted into a role he hadn't envisaged for

himself so soon in life. A man who loved a good evening of drinks, KB would join the young officers for a round of the tipple at the end of a hard day.[7] In fact, the 7th Battalion was sometimes criticized for encouraging a culture of drinking among youngsters and KB occasionally found himself at the receiving end of such snide remarks. But his bonding time with the greenhorns of the 7th Battalion gave him great confidence in their potential.

One of the youngsters in KB's battalion was Narayan Parulekar. In the aftermath of the 1962 war several young men in India joined the army as officers inducted through a fast-track route called the emergency commission.[8] These young men had followed the war on the radio, listening intently to stories of the bravery of soldiers who gave up their lives in the conflict.

Narayan Parulekar, or Paru, was working with the Bombay Port Trust at that time. Like many others, he answered the call of duty to the nation and applied for an emergency commission as an officer.[9] He was commissioned into the newly raised the 7th Battalion which KB now commanded.

Paru, the first adjutant of the battalion, was also given the charge of a rifle company. An adjutant of the battalion is the staff officer to the commanding officer of the battalion and assists the commanding officer in operational planning, induction, training and utilization of troops in a battalion.[10] Though an adjutant is an appointment manned by a senior captain or a major, Paru was a newly appointed captain.[11] He was also given charge of one of the four companies in the battalion (in 1967, a battalion had four rifle companies under it. A rifle company, comprising three platoons with a strength of around 130 personnel each, was commanded by a company commander who was usually a major. In 7/11 Gorkha Rifles those days, there was a paucity of captains and majors.) Alongside KB and Paru, there were several young officers from different parts of India, with backgrounds that were varied and interesting. One of them was Lieutenant Ram Singh Rathore, a devout Rajput officer from Rajasthan with a fondness for weapons, who also played a key role in the battle of Cho La.[12]

In his new, expanded role as the commanding officer, KB would also spend time walking from one post to the other at Cho La, visiting his company commanders and men, taking mental notes of any trace of advantage the landscape afforded. He had to think like a battalion commander – how he could best motivate his officers, decide who would be the most suitable to lead a raid or attack, and so on. He believed his young battalion would rise to the occasion when the moment arrived.

While the commissioned officers in a battalion came from various parts of the country, the soldiers were drawn from a more defined community or region. In this battalion of 7/11 Gorkha Rifles, the troops mostly came from the Rai and Limbu tribes that lived in the rugged, severe terrain of eastern Nepal – where men were known as much for their ferocity as for their quick temper. While the officers would gather for a drink in the evenings, the officers and 'men' would only get an opportunity to socially mingle with each other at community meals such as barakhanas – grand feasts for the troops to promote camaraderie between soldiers and officers in a battalion. In remote areas such as Cho La where troops were isolated for long periods of time, which was mentally and emotionally challenging, a barakhana was an occasion to strengthen bonds, revitalize spirits and rejuvenate physical energies before returning to their posts. On such occasions the forward positions of battalions would be substituted by others.

As mentioned earlier, the soldiers of 7/11 Gorkhas hadn't served in the field before. They were struggling to become familiar with the Ishapore rifle – a weapon that had recently been inducted into the Indian army. There had been limited issues of the rifles in 17 Division. Local training cadres were organized within the division to familiarize the boys with new weapons such as the rifles. They practised in makeshift firing ranges. Most of the boys, however, continued to use the old rifles. Whenever vacancies arose, a few would be sent to attend military courses to train on new, more specialized weapons the army had inducted as part of the scramble to furbish itself with modern weapons after the debacle of 1962. Mhow (Military Headquarters of War), a cantonment town founded in 1818 near village Mahu in Madhya Pradesh, had become one of the Indian army's best-equipped operational training establishments.

Among those who arrived at the Infantry School in Mhow to attend the gun course in the summer of 1967 was Havildar Tinjong Lama of 7/11 Gorkhas – a short, burly lad from the hills of Lamahatta, near Darjeeling. When his commanding officer sent him to Mhow for the Recoilless Gun[13] (RCL) course, Tinjong, who had not attended secondary school, could not read or write proficiently. Yet, the irrepressible lad from the Bhutia tribe simply wouldn't give up and studied hard, long after the day's training was over to attain a good grade. The instructor noticed the skilled manner in which Tinjong handled the weapon, though he struggled to get marks in the theory section of the course. He soon picked up nuances about the use of the weapon in higher altitudes such as Sikkim.[14] When Tinjong returned to Sikkim after the course, he was one of the few qualified weapon experts in the battalion.

One of Tinjong's colleagues in the 7th Battalion was Rifleman Debi Prasad, who came from a modest background in Nepal like most other boys who had been recruited from the hills. Debi would routinely unsheathe his khukri and twirl the weapon in his hand. It was a tool he had trusted from his teenage years when he roamed the lonely forests near his village; the cold steel of the dagger in his hand filled him with the confidence to overcome adversity. Young boys like Debi came from villages in eastern Nepal, having grown up on stories about soldiering in faraway lands that involved roaming the jungles, scaling mountains and exploring forests in natty uniforms. He had heard legendary tales of the Gurkhas in the Second World War – some of them from his Limbu village – such as how a brigade full of Gurkhas took out the famed 48 Division of Japanese troops in Burma – after the latter had defeated 1,30,000 British and Australian troops in Singapore. In a counterattack at Kyaukse, they lost ten men and killed 500 Japanese troops[15] and earned the title of 'bravest of the brave'. Since the time of the Raj, soldiering was a badge of honour that took the boys to Africa and Europe – and this tradition of recruiting Nepalis into the Indian army continued in independent India. Debi and others like him wanted to fight, like every soldier, and maybe win an honour one day if he fought well. Just like his heroes – Gaje Ghale and Ganju Lama – both Victoria Cross awardees from the Second World War in the

1940s. The newly issued 7.62 mm Ishapore rifle slung over his shoulder, a khukri by his side, Debi knew his turn would come.

~

Another battalion that played a key role in 1967 and arrived in Sikkim around that time was 2nd Grenadiers. While 11 Gorkha Rifles was one of the youngest regiments, the Grenadiers was amongst the oldest in the Indian army. In fact the 3rd Grenadiers battalion, led by Lieutenant Colonel V.P. Airy, fought a fascinating battle at Jarpal against a Pakistani battalion led by Lieutenant Colonel Akram Raza.

The Pakistani soldiers, under the intrepid Akram Raza, proved hard to overcome and put up a tough fight. Despite being finally defeated by Indian forces, Raza fought valiantly and led his troops with such ferocity that he won the admiration and respect of the Indian forces. By the time Raza died fighting the Indian army, he had proved himself to be the true hero of the battle of Jarpal. Lieutenant Colonel Airy admired the bravery of his counterpart and shot off a handwritten note to the Pakistani army headquarters praising Raza's bravery. Based on Airy's note, Pakistan awarded Raza the Nishan-e-Haider, Pakistan's highest honour. It was one of the rare instances in history when a soldier had won a country's highest honour based on a citation drafted by an enemy commander who had watched him fight from the other side. The Grenadiers had acquired a name for themselves not only on account of their bravery but for their noble conduct on the battlefield as well.[16] The 2nd Grenadiers, posted in Sikkim in the mid-1960s, had an impressive history of its own in battles over the previous two hundred years. The battalion had earned laurels fighting against Napoleon in Egypt in 1801, in the Third Anglo-Maratha War in 1808, the first Afghan War in 1840 and in the First World War. The 2nd Grenadiers was part of an elite regiment of the Indian army which had the unique distinction of being among the largest secular forces in the world. The regiment had Ahirs, Dogras, Gujars, Muslims, Rajputs, Jats, Kaim Khanis, Kutchis and Saurashtrians, Meenas and others. Lieutenant Colonel Rai Singh helmed the battalion which occupied the defences at Nathu La in Sikkim. Hardy and ebullient as a kid, Rai Singh had enrolled in the army as a sepoy in 1944, before his twentieth birthday.

In 1945 the Grenadiers regiment, which had been known as the Bombay Grenadiers then, was redesignated Indian Grenadiers. It was assigned to India around the time of Independence. Rai applied and became a commissioned officer in 1950. Ambitious and forever keen to learn about military tactics and warfare, Rai did well as a young officer and was chosen to attend the prestigious Defence Services Staff College course at Camberley in England.[17] The 2nd Grenadiers that arrived in Sikkim was a mix of calm, unflappable company commanders such as Bishan Singh and intrepid youngsters such as P.S. Dagar. Rai, Bishan Singh and Dagar all played critical roles in the battle of Nathu La in 1967.

~

Meanwhile, along the watershed, tensions had mounted in the period between 1965 and 1967. Often, Chinese spokespersons would invoke the 'lessons of 1962' to remind India about the possible result that awaited it in case the two armies clashed again. Patrols, commonly called 'Billy patrols', that walked along the border often clashed, resulting in casualties.[18] The key source of the dispute was the precise location of the border, which was unmarked. The Indian government asserted the watershed principle to determine the border.[19] The correct border, they stated, was the ridgeline (or drain) that ran along these passes and marked their deepest points. But as the border was not marked – and an expansionist and aggressive China wanted to creep into and grab Indian territory – Peking was wrongly trying to claim several vantage points on the watershed.[20]

China's psychological pressure and aggression had caused India's withdrawal at Jelep La in 1965. But an adamant posture in Nathu La – thanks to Sagat – meant that India didn't vacate the watershed along the crest and the two countries' armies were pitted against each other in a potential face-off.

6

The Tipping Point:
A Tale of Spies and a Breach
at the Watershed

For twenty-six-year-old Krishnan Raghunath, Peking was
a window to discover China. As a teenager growing up
in India, Raghunath had lived through the heady days of
the 1950s when slogans of 'Hindi–Chini bhai bhai' rent
the air. In his early youth in the 1960s the war ended
all bonhomie between the two countries. So, as a young
foreign service officer, a posting as the second secretary at
the Indian embassy in Peking in 1965 was an opportunity
to better understand China. At the embassy he was
heading the Information Services of India (ISI). Among
ISI's challenges was to cope with the restrictions on
exchange of information that the communist government
posed for them in China.[1]

June was the beginning of the summer season in Peking. Midsummer rains would pelt the city every time the temperatures rose. 4 June 1967 began as any other regular day for Raghunath. At the hour past midday, he settled into his car along with his colleague P. Vijai and set off towards the Western Hills to visit the temple of the Sleeping Buddha.[2] Along the way, a curious Raghunath noticed the decrepit remains of another temple and stopped the car. He fished out his camera and began to take pictures of it. As he looked through the aperture of his camera to take more shots, he felt a light tap on his shoulder.

A bystander asked him why he was taking pictures in a sensitive military zone where photography was prohibited. Before Raghunath could realize what was happening, the two Indian diplomats were surrounded by soldiers of the PLA. A harried Raghunath tried to reason with the people around him that he did not mean to take photographs for any spying purposes and that he was only interested in the ruins of the temple. The Chinese, however, believed that Raghunath was using the pretext of the temple nearby to click pictures in a prohibited military zone. Upon inspection, their identity cards as embassy staffers were confiscated. The two were whisked into a vehicle and taken away. That evening, news broke about the unprecedented arrest of two Indian diplomats by Chinese authorities.

The Indian embassy immediately swung into action. The diplomats had been accused by China of spying. Denials followed and clarifications were issued that they had not indulged in any espionage activities. But China maintained that Raghunath and Vijai were taking illicit pictures in a sensitive area that had a prohibited military facility close by. The Ministry of Foreign Affairs in Peking alleged that the diplomats had been trying to create a topographical map of a 'prohibited area'.[3] According to the Chinese, 'Upon discovering them, soldiers of the Chinese PLA guarding the area immediately urged them to desist and asked them to leave. K. Raghunath and P. Vijai, however, paid no heed whatsoever and continued to hang around and take photographs of the prohibited area stealthily.' The Chinese government withdrew Krishnan Raghunath's diplomatic status and declared Vijai a persona non grata.[4]

Over a week later, on 13 June, about 15,000 people gathered at the Peking Municipal People's Higher Court for the trial of the two Indian diplomats accused of spying on China. Raghunath and Vijai were 'tried' and found guilty of espionage. Raghunath was sentenced to 'immediate deportation'[5] by the court and told to leave the country forthwith, while Vijai was given three days to leave China. However, despite the different orders, they were brought to the airport at Peking the following morning where an irate mob awaited them. Red Guards kicked and punched the Indian diplomats. A cordon of members of the Indian embassy staff who tried to protect them were also assaulted. Raghunath was forced to walk through a jeering mob of Red Guards, who jostled, kicked and spat on him. Vijai was dragged with his head shoved down, his shoes tearing off in the melee.[6] The humiliation of the two diplomats was meant to send a loud message to India: beware.

In Delhi, the news gave rise to shock and anger and was received with angry protests from political parties. The Indian government believed that the Chinese government had violated international norms by making a film on the confessions of two Indian diplomats for use as propaganda against Indian espionage in China.[7] The Jana Sangh, which was trying to cultivate a muscular Hindu Indian identity, seized the opportunity to try to press the government into a corner. China had thrown down the gauntlet to India's young prime minister who had built up an early reputation for a certain kind of decisiveness that swung between foolhardiness and brilliant audacity. Indira Gandhi would respond soon.

In response to the Chinese belligerence, Chen Lu-Chih, the first secretary of the Chinese embassy in New Delhi, was accused of gathering vital intelligence from India and carrying on subversive activities on Indian soil.[8] Chen was stripped of his diplomatic immunity and ordered to register under the Foreigners' Registration Act.

Unlike China, India didn't bother with a trial. The next day, on 14 June, the external affairs ministry ordered his immediate deportation to China.[9] The government now turned towards Hsieh Cheng-Hao, who was the third secretary of the embassy, and accused him of subversive activities too. He was promptly declared persona non grata and ordered to leave India within seventy-two hours. The Indian government had responded with alacrity and unusual boldness, showing the heart to return China's compliment. By now public emotions were riled up. The very next day after the deportation order, crowds gathered outside the Chinese embassy in Delhi, demonstrating vociferously as political parties pounced on the opportunity, instigating mobs to break into the embassy compound and go on a rampage. The mob smashed windows, set fire to a garage, tore down the Chinese flag and assaulted members of the embassy staff. That day seven members of the embassy staff, including Chen Lu-Chih and Hsieh Cheng-Hao, had to be taken to hospital.[10]

The attack on the Chinese embassy set off alarms in Peking. Taking serious note of the violence in Delhi,

Mob carrying an effigy gets restive during the protest in Delhi.

A man throwing a potted plant inside the embassy
during the protest.

Hindustan Times

An injured Chinese diplomat rescued from the
mob under heavy security.

Hindustan Times

A scared Chinese staffer inside the embassy during the protest.

An ambulance for the staffers arrives at the Chinese embassy.

the Chinese government sent a notice to Ram Sathe, the Indian charge d'affaires in Peking, that the Indian embassy staff's safety could no longer be guaranteed. Protesters soon gathered outside Sathe's residence, tearing down the windows of his house, sending the occupants scurrying for safety. The Indian embassy was also under siege with sixty-three men, women and children holed up inside. The hostility on both sides had crossed diplomatic lines. The danger to the lives of the diplomats on both sides was beginning to raise international concern. The likelihood of another war loomed dangerously close.

In Peking, Western diplomats rushed to intervene and decided to deliver food to the persons trapped inside the Indian embassy. But the Western food convoy was turned back by the Red Guards and the police.

India sent a note that unless the siege was lifted, 'appropriate counter measures' would be adopted. Armed sentries arrived at the Chinese embassy in New Delhi the following day with specific instructions for the Chinese diplomats: the occupants were ordered not to leave the building. India was not about to back off, even if it meant that the embassy staff in both countries ended up being detained as prisoners.

Looking for a possible detente, the Chinese foreign ministry suggested sending an aircraft to Delhi to bring back their diplomats injured in the attack in Delhi. The

Indian government responded with a similar request for its diplomats holed up in Peking. China, however, turned down their request. But they didn't seem to anticipate that India was in no mood to capitulate. The following day, as a Chinese aircraft touched down in Delhi to take back the diplomats, the government in Delhi refused to provide refuelling facilities for the aircraft. Finally, after assurances, an injured Hsieh Cheng-Hao was allowed to leave Delhi on 21 June. Chen Lu-Chih was kept under detention and deported three days later.

The demonstrations outside the Indian embassy in Peking, somewhat staged, were called off soon after. Sathe was told that the embassy staff were free to leave the compound and return to their flats. The Indians responded with a reciprocal gesture and withdrew their sentries at the Chinese embassy. The staff could now step out of the embassy in Delhi, though their personal safety remained unguaranteed.

India had matched China for every stride and even outwitted the adversary on occasions. After having mirrored each other's unyielding and harsh steps, peace overtures from both sides also started to mimic each other. An uneasy truce was established and the ugly diplomatic fracas didn't blow up into a military crisis. The bickering, though, resumed when the Chinese embassy accused Indian customs of seizing literature that contained Mao

Zedong's works. The Indian government, their note complained, was preventing the Chinese staff from their right to study Mao's thought. To the Chinese, this was the larger conspiracy of capitalism at play.

The rivalry between India and China had begun to worry the West. The diplomatic stand-off had attracted international attention and shortly manifested itself on the border. As if on cue, attention turned to the tiny Himalayan outpost of Nathu La.

Since 1965 the Chinese had been attempting to dominate the border by various means. They used to make regular broadcasts from loudspeakers at Nathu La, pointing out to Indian troops the pathetic conditions in which they lived, their low salaries and lack of amenities, comparing them to those enjoyed by Chinese officers. Sagat had loudspeakers installed on the Indian side and played similar messages in Chinese every day. Throughout 1966 and early 1967, Chinese propaganda, intimidation and attempted incursions into Indian territory continued. As mentioned earlier, the border was not marked and there were several vantage points on the watershed which both sides thought belonged to them. Patrols which walked along the border often clashed, resulting in tension, and sometimes even casualties.[11]

~

In the first week of August 1967, the 2nd Battalion of the Grenadiers moved up to occupy the border outposts at Nathu La, replacing the outgoing battalion. Led by Lieutenant Colonel Rai Singh, the battalion consisted mostly of soldiers from India's northern belt of Haryana and Rajasthan. Major Bishan Singh had around three years of service when he took over as 'Tiger Nathu La', the moniker for the company commander holding the actual pass. Bishan was joined by a younger, energetic captain, P.S. Dagar, as his second in command.

The terrain features guided the way Rai Singh positioned the battalion: straddling the key points in the area. Bishan's company at Nathu La spread its platoons across nearby features, some of the names derived from the silhouettes they made on the sky, such as Camel's Back, South Shoulder, Centre Bump and the indigenously named Sebu La. The battalion headquarters were set up below the actual pass at a rear post named Gole Ghar,[12] where Rai Singh, as the commanding officer of the battalion, was positioned, while the 3-inch mortars were close to Sherathang (which was a hundred metres away behind Nathu La), which also had the administrative base and forward aid post.

When the Grenadiers battalion took over the defences at Nathu La, the activities on the Chinese side increased. They began to repair their bunker at North Shoulder,

First news of Chinese soldiers at Nathu La that appeared
in the Indian newspapers.

which was inside Chinese territory, built new ones and moved more troops inside them. They increased their show of aggressive postures in the area. On 13 August 1967, ten–twelve Chinese soldiers marched ominously towards the watershed, crossed over to the Indian side and audaciously began to dig trenches in Indian territory. Indian troops arrived at the spot and the Chinese responded by filling up the trenches and going back. The Chinese believed that the loudspeaker propaganda was successful and added eight more loudspeakers, bringing the total number to twelve. Nathu La came to resemble a cricket stadium in Bombay.

The Indians hurried to respond and heaved up 30 watt amplifiers with six speakers to South Shoulder. Pre-recorded propaganda was relayed through these loudspeakers, the sounds reverberating over the mountains, unsettling its quietude. This may even have been thought of as amusing and ridiculous, if not for the attendant threat that lurked underneath. A team of reporters arrived from the magazine *Times Life* to cover the drama at Nathu La and spent time taking pictures of soldiers on either side of the watershed border. The goings-on in the area made for excellent news, with the soldiers trying to outshout each other. It was a boxing match for an anteroom audience.

India, under Indira Gandhi, hadn't baulked at the

Colonel Bishan Singh (retd)

Portrait of Mao Zedong placed near the observation post
on the Chinese side. It was only twenty yards from Indian
defences and was closely guarded by Chinese troops.

constant Chinese threats and had stood up to the pressure.
One day, the Indians decided to raise the ante. Rai
Singh declared that his battalion would celebrate India's
Independence Day on 15 August next to the Nehru Stone.
(In 1959, India's first prime minister had undertaken
a trip to Bhutan: the stone, a feature on the Nathu La
watershed, symbolized the point from where his trip had
begun.) For the Chinese, the gathering of Indians next
to the watershed line was both irksome and alarming.

As a hundred Grenadiers troops began to gather next
to the stone for the puja (infantry battalions in the army
start endeavours with a ceremony called the mandir
parade) in the morning, the Chinese frantically huddled
in their bunkers – boots laced up, caps on heads, weapons

ready to be primed and baffled eyes rooted to the spot where the priests stood chanting mantras.

But the skirmishes and pressure-cooker environment had begun to cause concern in the higher headquarters on the Indian side. Sagat, commander of 17 Mountain Division, under whose jurisdiction the area lay (under 17 Division operated 112 Brigade. The Grenadiers was a part of 112 Brigade), decided to seek out his boss, Lieutenant General Jagjit Aurora, the corps commander, and take his approval to mark the international boundary according to the watershed principle. Sagat's plan would mark the beginning of a violent turn of events. Months ago, while moving up to Nathu La with his battalion to occupy defences, Rai Singh had met Sagat at the divisional headquarters. Sagat's advice to him was to get his men trained to lay barbed wire. At that time, Rai hadn't quite understood what Sagat had in mind, but when instructions arrived from the division headquarters about laying barbed wire along the border, Rai knew exactly what Sagat had had in mind months ago.

On 20 August, Rai Singh's battalion began to lay a barbed wire fence to mark the border with China. No sooner had the work begun than the Chinese loudly demanded the Indians to stop. Unmindful, the Indians continued to lay the fence as the Chinese watched agitatedly. Something was going to give soon.

Three days later, Bishan Singh, the company commander at Nathu La, was looking forward to a lazy, relaxed afternoon. While chatting with a couple of his boys, he noticed a bunch of Chinese soldiers streaming towards the watershed border which had not yet been fully demarcated with a barbed wire fence. There were twenty, thirty, forty, fifty, maybe more, he counted. The rifleman next to him counted seventy-five Chinese soldiers advancing towards the watershed.[13] Kitted in battle gear, rifles unslung and ready, fitted with bayonets aimed at the Indians, their faces were serious, their eyes gleaming. Bishan hollered for the troops to get ready.

The line of Chinese soldiers began to grow longer as the Indians watched with bated breath, their hearts in their mouths. When the soldiers reached the watershed border, the line of Chinese soldiers suddenly stopped advancing, as if checked by an unseen forcefield. Before the frozen men stood an enthusiastic political commissar, the political appointee in every army battalion of the PLA. The commissar flipped open a red book and began to read sermons of communism. The troops obediently recited after him. Bishan was ready, his hands wrapped around his weapon, his soldiers awaiting orders to fight. Bishan immediately sensed all hell would break loose if fighting were to start. He waited to see what the Chinese would do next but nothing happened for a while. No one

Colonel Bishan Singh (retd)

The Chinese political commissar was a key interlocutor at Nathu La. He is far right in the picture along with the commanding officer of their battalion.

moved, no one fired. Incredibly enough, the Chinese made the first move – they returned to their bunkers. Bishan and his men heaved a sigh of relief.

The Chinese had retreated to their bunkers but left behind a few doubts in Bishan's mind. What would have happened had the Chinese soldiers marched across? Should he have asked his men to fire? What would have happened if he had ordered his men to open fire? What if the Chinese had crossed over – all seventy-five of them – and not fired at all? Should he still have fired? What was that precise point at which a crossing became a crossing? What was the point at which China was no longer China but India, Indian soil? The unmarked parts of the watershed border were a source of constant confusion.

The situation at Nathu La was swiftly deteriorating. Sagat, the division commander, and Jagjit Aurora, the corps commander, chose to see the situation first hand. On 1 September, when the two arrived at Nathu La, the visibility was dismal. The two commanders along with their support staff strode towards the key features in the area – first the Centre Bump and then towards South Shoulder before walking along the Four Poles area, where they decided to take a few steps north. That meant stepping inside Chinese territory. No sooner had they taken a few steps than the Chinese political commissar along with a few boys rushed towards them. 'Chini Chini!' the commissar screamed, trying to indicate that they were inside China. The two generals withdrew at once, but the commissar and his men continued to grumble. He called a photographer and made him take pictures of the footsteps of the generals on Chinese soil.

The generals returned to the battalion base that afternoon but Sagat knew the issue wasn't closed and that he needed to stay ahead of the Chinese. The next morning, he returned to the Nathu La post with a plan. He directed that a patrol be sent out along the unmarked border towards Camel's Back on the Indian side. Bishan set out with a team of one junior commissioned officer (junior commissioned officers, or JCOs, are soldiers who join the army as sepoys or riflemen at the lowest rung and rise through several promotions to become JCOs) and fifteen soldiers.[14] Rai Singh, the commanding officer of the battalion, and his team kept themselves ready on South Shoulder for any eventuality. On the way, the patrol was intercepted by a group of Chinese soldiers. Bishan tried to explain that they were inside Indian territory and that it was the Chinese who had stepped out of bounds. But within moments, Bishan and his men found themselves surrounded by a number of Chinese soldiers. Both sides, armed and evenly matched, began to jostle and push each other. Rai Singh kept an eye on the two groups from close by. Miraculously, again, no one opened fire. Bishan and his team soon returned to the company headquarters.

The questions that were bothering Bishan earlier had begun to trouble Sagat too. How could the soldiers protect Indian soil if the border itself was unmarked, especially so when Chinese troops had been repeatedly violating the border over the last few years. India believed that the watershed line marked the boundary. But the Chinese, on the other hand, even contested the mere presence of the Indian army in Sikkim. Sagat believed he was right to have started the project of marking out the border according to the watershed principle. The line that separated China and Sikkim would have to be marked out explicitly, once and for all.

~

A blistering cold breeze greeted the Indian soldiers at the watershed line at Nathu La in the early morning of 5 September. They began to build a fence along the border using concertina coils unpacked from boxes. The Chinese were ready and both sides were spoiling for another quarrel. This time, the Chinese political commissar stood facing the dogged commanding officer, Rai Singh. Work had to be stopped at 8 a.m. as the impasse between the two sides couldn't be broken. That night, a desperate Chinese patrol crept up to South Shoulder and dug up a portion of it. When the Indians went to restart the work on the barbed wire the next morning, the Chinese were ready and waiting for them with buckets of water. By digging at the top of the ridge they had altered the slope

The wire fence being built at Nathu La while
a Chinese soldier watches.

Lieutenant Colonel Rai Singh, commanding officer, the 2nd
Grenadiers, and Adjutant Captain B.S. Koshal explaining to agitated
Chinese soldiers the alignment of barbed wire along the watershed.

of the watershed and therefore the position of the border. As soon as the Indians arrived the Chinese emptied the buckets on the slope of the altered bump to indicate the new watershed line.

On 7 September, a hundred Chinese soldiers again appeared at the flattish site of the fence. The quarrel grew into a brawl that day. The two sides launched into each other, throwing fists and mouthing abuses – though no side understood the other's language.

The Jats, taller and bigger, swung hard at the Chinese while the nimbler soldiers of the PLA proved equal to

Soldiers from both sides facing off during the arguments over the fence.

the task. The rotund, fleshy Chinese political commissar joined in and tried to intervene. The commissar was a senior official in the Chinese hierarchy and the Chinese expected his presence to calm the Jats down. Instead, miffed by his continued interference and haughtiness, one of the Indian soldiers pounced on the commissar, pulled him by the scruff of his neck and pushed him hard. The commissar fell to the ground, and ended up with smashed glasses and a broken nose. This unbelievable insult to a senior Chinese official deeply upset the PLA soldiers and they joined in numbers to take on the Jats. By the time the fracas ended, both sides had a few wounded and bruised. The Indians claimed to have got the better of the Chinese when the latter had in fact succeeded in preventing the Indians from continuing with their fence work.

A compromise on the issue had proved difficult between the two cantankerous sides in the absence of any reasonable communication. Neither side was about to step down from their extreme positions.

It was the final warning that a bunch of men with weapons in a remote Himalayan ridge might run out of patience despite their military training to restrain their instincts about opening up with their weapons. The incident with the commissar was something that the Chinese were unlikely to forget easily.

At that moment, Sagat sat grappling with a strange dilemma. He realized that the dogged Chinese wouldn't let the Grenadiers troops lay the wire. If he failed now, it would be a loss of face. If he tried to persist, there could be another scrap. The fight could end up in a serious armed confrontation. But Sagat was determined to complete the barbed wire fence and put an end to the confusion about the border.[15]

On the night of 10 September, Division Commander Sagat called an urgent meeting at the headquarters of 112 Mountain Brigade (commanded by Brigadier M.M.S. Bakshi) in Chhanggu. The officers were told to be ready if the situation got out of hand. Bishan Singh was given the charge of laying the wire fence with P.S. Dagar as his assistant. Additional men, such as from the Engineers Regiment, and material were moved for this purpose. The artillery, who had been brought up earlier, were also told to be ready. The long meeting ended at midnight.

Rai Singh looked up at the sky as he stepped out of the meeting. There was no star in sight: it was pitch dark.

Lieutenant General Sagat Singh (front row, third from right)
with officers and troops at Nathu La, 1967.

Lieutenant General Sagat Singh (right) with Brigadier Bakshi,
the brigade commander in Sikkim.

7

Hellfire at Nathu La

On the night of 10 September, Sagat Singh got little sleep. He would soon know whether or not he had taken the right decision by insisting on the fencing of the border. More stores were moved to Nathu La for laying the fence the next morning. Bishan Singh and P.S. Dagar were in charge of laying the fence, which was under the supervision of Rai Singh, the 2nd Grenadiers' commanding officer. A detailed communication plan was drawn up connecting the key geographical points in a potential skirmish. The plan was to lay wires and establish audio links via field telephones (which run on inbuilt batteries) to sustain uninterrupted transmission of instructions in battle conditions. A new signal wireline was thus laid overnight from the brigade headquarters (in

Chhanggu, the venue of the meeting of 10 September) to Sherathang (a couple of kilometres away from Nathu La) where the mortars[1] were stored and which was the administrative base for the 2nd Grenadiers. The network of lines was then patched to the division headquarters.

Brigadier Bakshi, the brigade commander, was an armoured corps officer who specialized in tank warfare in the plains and didn't possess experience in the Himalayas, where tanks didn't have a role to play. For his role in the 1965 war, he was awarded the Maha Vir Chakra, one of the nation's eminent gallantry awards. Bakshi was asked to move up from the brigade headquarters in Chhanggu and occupy the forward post at Nathu La. On his part, Division Commander Sagat Singh decided to relocate to the brigade headquarters. Clearly, Sagat wanted to be close to the point of action. Anticipating an aggressive Chinese response, on Sagat's instructions, he had ordered Rai Singh to move from Gole Ghar, the site of the battalion headquarters, to the forward post at Nathu La, close to the area of fencing, to oversee the progress while Bishan and Dagar led their men to work on the fence. During his briefing, Sagat made it clear that Rai Singh needed to stay under cover inside the bunker and not expose himself. The wily general had thought out the various possibilities to the last detail.

As planned, Brigadier Bakshi left for Nathu La at 5

a.m. on 11 September. Accompanying him was Naveen Gupta, the young signal officer tasked to handle the communication at Nathu La. The artillery observation post officers at Sebu La and Camel's Back had been put on alert.

Sheru Thapliyal had grown up in the hills of Garhwal, and was inspired by Major Shaitan Singh, a hero of the 1962 war.[2] At the end of his training course in 1967, he was commissioned into the artillery regiment, which was a part of 112 Brigade,[3] and arrived on his first posting in Sikkim. He was placed at the artillery observation post at Sebu La, an elevated feature beside Nathu La that overlooked the pass. From Sebu La, a soldier would have a clear view of the entire Chinese defence, including the feature known as North Shoulder (on the Chinese side), the stretch of the Yatung valley that lay behind the defence and the roads that snaked up from the Yatung valley to the forward posts and enabled vehicles to bring stores and troops from the rear.

Sheru was aware of the work on the fence at the border and the ongoing tussle kept him on his toes. As an artillery observation post officer, his role was to bring down heavy fire and shelling on the enemy. Ahead of him lay craggy hill features stretched in the far distance and the gently rolling Yatung valley in Tibet on the Chinese side. Along with his fellow artillery officer on the other

141

flank, Sheru enjoyed a clear view of China's depth areas. It seemed like a special position for him from where he could watch over the enemy country like an eagle sitting on a ledge. Unlike him, the Chinese did not have a similar view into India from their artillery position on North Shoulder.

Sagat, in his briefing the previous evening, had unequivocally instructed his commanders not to expose themselves to the enemy. As the wire-laying party headed by Bishan Singh and Dagar walked out in the open, the rest of them – Sheru and his boys on Sebu La, Brigade Commander M.M.S. Bakshi along with his signal officer, Naveen, a little distance away on the elevated area of the Central Bump – watched with bated breath. In spite of Sagat's explicit instructions to stay inside his bunker at Nathu La, Rai Singh couldn't just sit and watch his boys face the enemy. As the wire-laying party under Bishan set off to work on the fence, Rai Singh instinctively stepped out from the trenches along with an armed escort and joined them. Rai Singh, Bishan, Dagar and the other designated boys were now out in the open.

Work commenced at dawn as planned. The response was an expected one too – a bunch of Chinese soldiers, eager for the Indians to show up, strode up angrily to the fence. The PLA men stood in front of the soldiers laying the wire. The Chinese commander was leading the argument and the political commissar stood next to him facing Rai Singh and the others including Bishan and his men. The Indians were asked to stop work immediately. Patience, clearly, was running out faster than expected.

Naveen had a good view of the wire laying activity and later wrote how 'there was quite a lot of shouting going on. We had around 120 men involved in the fence laying. They were working in small teams at around six points on the slope and the pass. The Chinese had around 150 troops opposing the wire laying and there was pushing and heckling going on between the two sides. Barring the commotion and despite the opposition things seemed to be moving as planned and the fence appeared to be getting into position.'4

A scuffle erupted and the commissar got roughed up once again. Then, all of a sudden, the Chinese soldiers disengaged and returned to their bunkers. They acted with chilling, unflappable coordination. Gone was the sulkiness of previous occasions. The Indians were taken aback. The wire laying party stood there, baffled at the unexpected turn, and then proceeded to continue their work. It all returned to being quiet, but only for a while.

On the Chinese side, the morning was going as per plan. The commissar and the party had returned to their bunkers, leaving the Indians uncertain and uneasy. Their machine guns had been put in place, the gunners had been alerted, the soldiers in their bunkers had taken position. The entire unit was ready, in stand-to position. The machine gunners inside the bunkers picked their aims. The watershed line bore the silhouettes of busy men with long iron pickets. The Chinese soldiers awaited the signal. It was due any moment.

It was around 7.45 a.m. when a loud whistle broke the silence. What followed was the unbroken, grating, terrifying staccato of machine-gun fire. The Chinese let loose a ruthless barrage of shots on the exposed fence-laying Indian party.

Rai Singh slumped, felled by the first volley that spat out of the Chinese bunkers, and was out of commission for the rest of the battle. The guns roared louder and the gunfire picked out more Indians in the open. It was a pitiful massacre. The horrifying sight of fellow soldiers dropping next to each other or watching their heads blown apart struck horror among the Indians.

In the initial barrage a hundred men, caught out in the open, perished or were injured, including a few Chinese who were tardy in getting into their bunkers. With their commanding officer Rai Singh shot at the start, the Indian troops ran helter-skelter. The suddenness of the Chinese actions had forced a bunch of soldiers, over thirty according to accounts, to instinctively make a run for their lives: some even escaping from the scene. This unpleasant chapter of the battle is often dropped from narrations, but to exclude this would undermine the heroism of the soldiers who stood and fought gallantly. Months later, court martials would be held to prosecute deserters, on charges of cowardice.

A half hour into the firing, Naveen heard a sharp whistling sound overhead. Soon, the area was pounded by shelling. The Chinese opened up with their artillery. It wasn't long before the gunners made their adjustments and the shells began to inch closer to the Indian posts, raining hellfire from the sky. Something needed to be done quickly to salvage the situation. But why didn't the Indians counter-fire with their artillery guns? The devastating barrage of fire from the enemy bunkers had left the Indian side too shell-shocked to send an immediate response. They also required permission from the higher headquarters to use artillery. When the Indians responded by opening up with machine guns, the Chinese soldiers took positions inside their bunkers.

In the bunkers, Bakshi was aware that the morale of the troops would start to sink if an effective response wasn't mounted soon. Bishan Singh, the young company commander who was heading the fence-laying party, gathered his men for an appropriate riposte.

Meanwhile, Major Harbhajan (of 18 Rajput Regiment whose one platoon had been brought in from the nearby Yak La pass and deployed at Nathu La a few days earlier to reinforce the 2nd Grenadiers) had been in the bunkers all this while watching the episode unfold. The young daredevil major and his bunch charged towards the Chinese bunkers across the border, hoping to launch a physical assault from the front. Bishan didn't agree with this tactical plan and kept trying to deter them from following through with the plan. The Chinese bunkers were on higher ground. Harbhajan and his band of men had to run upslope to reach the fortifications. He knew it was going to be a kamikaze mission. Death was inevitable. Harbhajan and his men were cut down even before they could get close to the bunkers. Dagar followed with another bunch and met the same fate. They did, however, manage to shoot down a few Chinese before they were felled. Bishan, who had tried to prevent the two young officers from embarking on the suicidal mission,[5] provided covering fire to the young soldiers and even downed the Chinese soldier who shot Dagar. Bishan was also wounded in the process and fell unconscious, though he survived the battle, unlike Dagar and Harbhajan.[6] The Indian response was beaten back by the Chinese.

Sheru Thapliyal was sitting atop Sebu La, watching the action below. He saw Harbhajan and Dagar drop before his eyes. 'They couldn't have reached the Chinese bunkers anyway,' remembers Sheru with sadness. 'It was like a cruel movie playing before the eyes,' he recalls. Then the 'clouds rolled in and I couldn't see any more', Sheru reminisces fifty years later.[7]

As the Chinese firing intensified, Bakshi, who was at Central Bump, lost touch with the troops. Naveen remembers the chaos, 'By 0945 hours we had no contact with anyone on the position on the shoulders even on the artillery [radio] network. It was a panic situation for me. All the lines were down . . . There was no response on any of the almost dozen frequencies of the battalion in use that day.' Time was running out. Naveen realized he needed to get to the artillery officers at the observation posts soon if they had to launch a retaliation. He asked the radio operator at brigade headquarters to press in additional radio sets and string together a direct connection to Sheru Thapliyal, the artillery officer sitting on the higher feature, Sebu La.

Staying calm, the unflappable Bakshi felt that charging at the Chinese bunkers would result in more casualties. Bakshi moved out from his position at Central Bump and went around exhorting the men to keep fighting and not turn desperate. Signal Officer Naveen Gupta and Second Lieutenant Attar Singh, who were among the younger officers in the unit, joined in and ran from trench to trench as he yelled at the men to keep the flock together and respond with fire. The morale had to be kept up.

The signal line was relaid at Sherathang where Sagat had moved to.[8] He had asked his superiors for permission to use artillery support and the two artillery officers at the observation posts on Sebu La and Camel's Back had been asked by Sagat to be ready. Sagat needed approval from the army headquarters, which in turn needed the consent of the defence ministry. Such permission could take more than five hours to arrive. By then, the Chinese would gain an early advantage.

By then, signal communication with the platoon on South Shoulder had also been lost. On Bakshi's instructions, Naveen and a signal line repair party proceeded towards South Shoulder with a radio set for the platoon there. On arriving at the post, Naveen found the bodies of a few dead soldiers ahead of the defences. The post wore a desolate look as most men had either been killed or had left the post, barring an abandoned light machine gun (LMG). Naveen grabbed the LMG and fired a few salvos to show the post was still occupied. Bakshi radioed him that reinforcements were on their way and would take a while. To his relief, Naveen soon spotted Second Lieutenant Attar Singh and a group of soldiers coming down the slope, trying to rally the troops. The indefatigable Attar had continued to revive the men's spirits and managed to get some of them back on their feet and stay in the fight. In an unusual and unique episode, Attar would later be promoted by Sagat to the rank of captain on the spot, after he was told how the young officer restored the shocked spirits. The Grenadiers had suffered large numbers of casualties at the start, but the officers and men refused to back down and responded with machine guns and rifles. The melee continued amidst a gritty fightback from the Grenadiers.

As the fighting wore on, behind the ridge appeared a tall silhouette, ramrod straight in posture, a sten machine carbine in hand, at the back end of the battle. To the few that had had enough of the tough battle and who decided to retreat to a safer shelter, a rude surprise awaited. Sagat had decided to move closer to the scene of the battle. Like a no-nonsense army drill sergeant out to catch cadets who had loitered outside the precincts without permission, the general had started to marshal the troops that had abandoned the battle, shouting at them, herding them back into action.

Sagat stood on the road coming down from Nathu La trying to stem the rout. He even threatened to shoot anyone he found moving to the rear. Sagat hated to see his troops run away from the Chinese. When he saw a few men struggling to keep up, he screamed at them, scolding, lambasting those who had gone astray, finally collecting them like a schoolteacher at picnic and steering them back into class – up towards the forward posts, into their harnesses and back into the battle. Most of the soldiers stayed and fought valiantly, some attaining martyrdom. There were still a few who had deserted the battle that day. Over thirty soldiers faced court martial later for cowardice.[9]

Artillery officers sitting atop Sebu La and Camel's Back[10] could see deep into the Yatung valley,[11] as mentioned earlier. The dominant position overlooking Chinese territory provided them a clear line of sight. Communication had also been restored with them by then. Yet Sagat, sans permission from the government of India, hadn't been able to use artillery, in response to the Chinese shelling and heavy machine gun (HMG) fire that had cost him the lives of close to a hundred soldiers.

Sagat, in his capacity as a division commander, did not have the authority to use artillery and neither did the corps commander, Jagjit Singh Aurora. The army chief was away, travelling abroad, and Sam Manekshaw, the eastern army commander, who was officiating in his place in Delhi, wasn't immediately available to give the orders. Time was running out at Nathu La. Any more delay would have caused a repeat of 1962. When the higher-ups paid no heed to his insistence, as the commander on ground, Sagat Singh decided to order the artillery fire himself.

It is said that when Indira Gandhi, who was attending an important meeting, was finally asked for permission – though this was moot since Sagat had already ordered the use of artillery himself – she promptly gave the go-ahead. She took the message and ordered the use of artillery without hesitation.

The artillery officers in the observation posts, including Sheru, rose to the occasion. The medium guns boomed, supported by the machine guns and mortars from the forward posts. Sheru called up his cannons to unleash an uninterrupted torrent of bombardment on the Chinese, the shells crashing down on the Chinese bunkers. The road from the Yatung valley that brought supplies and reinforcements to the Chinese bunkers was shelled, causing immense damage to trucks and support elements. The Chinese soldiers, their bunkers, the support lines and communication had been wiped out.

By the time the bombardment ended, the casualties on the Chinese side were enormous. Approximately 340 PLA soldiers were dead and over 450 injured – bodies were strewn outside the bunkers, tossed behind the lines, buried in trenches.

The Chinese gunners had made the mistake of opening up, thus inviting the wrath of the better positioned Indian artillery. The Chinese shelling wasn't effective as the lay of the land ensured that most shells flew beyond the ridge and over the targets that sat in defiladed positions. But when the Indian artillery opened fire, it had every Chinese target within sight. The decimation of PLA defences, the first ever in a conflict in an India–China battle, was complete.

Sagat was a marked man because despite the success, casualties on the Indian side included eighty-eight dead and over 150 injured, which his superiors would not be happy about. An aggressive Sagat was not willing to take the setback lying down and he had even ordered Brigadier Bakshi to plan an attack on the Chinese on 13 September (the battle started on 11 September), as the continued artillery shelling had eliminated the Chinese defences. But the permission never came and the attack was shelved on orders from Delhi.[12]

On 14 September, the Chinese government threatened to use its air force if India continued with any more artillery shelling. It was evident that the Indian army had put the Chinese on the back foot and to tacitly accept that they had been soundly beaten in the battle of Nathu La. The Chinese now needed to up the ante – and hence the threat of using the air force. The lesson, though, had been driven home: the Chinese had been given a bloody nose. Fighting stopped thereafter at Nathu La.

The watershed remained on fire on either side from 11 to 14 September. When the firing and bombing finally stopped, the dead and the injured lay alongside each other, irrespective of where they belonged, ignoring claims of nationality; heavy smoke hung over the wreck, the mist occasionally uncovering horrifying sights of torn flesh and severed bodies that reeked of blood and gore. The conflict had claimed hundreds of lives but the count wasn't complete – there were bodies that lay down the ridge, behind the posts, across the border. Most were assumed dead but no one knew if there was a heart beating among them. Most of the injured didn't survive the freezing temperatures. Those, such as Rai Singh, who weathered gunshots at the beginning of the action, would suffer for the rest of their lives due to a few remaining pellets inside his body.

On 16 September, the bodies were handed over in a ceremony covered by the media and attended by Sam Manekshaw, Jagjit Singh Aurora and Sagat Singh.[13] Indian soldiers, in their retaliatory charge at the enemy bunkers, had lost their lives inside Chinese territory. Since the bodies had to be retrieved from inside their territory, the Chinese claimed that the Indians had attacked them.

Around that time, Morarji Desai, the Indian deputy prime minister and a veteran Indian politician, was visiting the US. On 13 September when Desai appeared on 'The Today Show', the Nathu La battle was on top of people's minds.

When asked about the Chinese warnings, Desai replied firmly, 'They are mainly angry about the fact that we are not submitting to their pressures and their bullying . . . They would like us to fall in line with their strategy or their policy of dominating Asia and, ultimately, the world, as I see it.'

When the clashes ended, American embassy officials reported back that 'Indians were confident they had the best of the incident.' There was a sense of relief within the US government and outside – not just that the clashes had remained limited, but also with regard to how India performed both militarily and diplomatically. There was an acknowledgement in the media, however, that India was better prepared than five years before.[14]

Stunned and alarmed, the Chinese, on the other side, were stewing over the losses and were bracing up for an opportunity to hit back. After all, Nathu La was likely to be an outlier, a spark in the dark. The Indians got lucky was the reaction of disbelief on the Chinese side.[11] For the Indian army that had been defeated over five years ago but had made a triumphant return at Nathu La, another stern test lay ahead.

8

The Battle of Cho La

The PLA hadn't expected India to open up with such incessant artillery pounding that inflicted heavy damage on the defences in their forward post at Nathu La. Unused to losing at the hands of Indians, a stunned PLA was smarting from the sudden setback. Due to the conflict at Nathu La the entire Sikkim–China border turned more vigilant and tense. Defences were strengthened across several locations on the Indian side for any possible flare-up.

7/11 Gorkha Rifles led by K.B. Joshi had spent two years in the area, with the last a few months being behind Nathu La, a little distance away from the line of action. Young officers and soldiers, in the reserves to be called up to support action at the border if needed, kept track of the action at Nathu La and kept themselves ready for deployment.

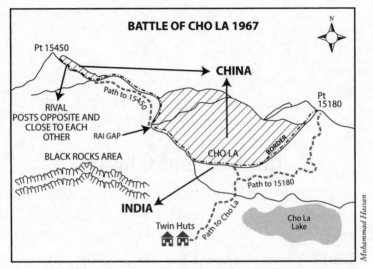

BATTLE OF CHO LA 1967

Pt 15450

RIVAL
POSTS OPPOSITE AND
CLOSE TO EACH
OTHER   RAI GAP

BLACK ROCKS AREA

Path to 15450

CHINA

Pt
15180

CHO LA

BORDER

Path to 15180

INDIA

Twin Huts

Path to Cho La

Cho La
Lake

Mohammad Hassan

This map is not to scale and is for explanatory purposes only. The international boundaries on the maps of India are neither purported to be correct nor authentic by Survey of India directives.

Cho La, a smaller pass in comparison with Nathu La, with a width of about 100 feet, was an anomalous piece of flatland amidst rocky cliffs that rose at its sides. Barren and devoid of any vegetation or cover, much of the area around Cho La was filled with craggy boulders and loose rocks that rendered movement in the area slow and difficult. 7/11 Gorkha Rifles was moved to another location in the area called Manla,[1] close to the Cho La pass. Unlike Nathu La, Cho La was not connected by usable roads. In order to prepare for battle, Sagat Singh had ordered that the culverts and gaps in the region be repaired. In and around the Cho La area were various posts whose defences were manned by two companies of the 10th Battalion of Jammu and Kashmir Rifles or 10 Jak Rif.[2]

Cho La was flanked on either side by two features on higher ground that dominated the area due to their elevations. On its west stood the higher of the two features and was called Point 15450, indicative of its height (in feet). The other feature, to the east of Cho La, was called Point 15180. Three Indian forward posts stood along the front of the border – occupying Point 15450, Cho La and Point 15180. Opposite each of these posts were positioned the forward posts of the Chinese army. At some places such as Point 15450, the troops on both sides were locked in an eyeball-to-eyeball confrontation with each other as the sentry posts of both Indian and Chinese forward posts at Point 15450 were sited barely 10 to 12 feet apart from each other. To the rear of these forward posts was a lower-lying area, where the Indian army had established posts called Tamze and Twin Huts, from where reinforcements could move up to the forward posts, if necessary

On 29 September, these two companies of 10 Jak Rif had to descend to the base in Chhanggu to celebrate a barakhana for troops planned on 1 October.

Two companies from 7/11 Gorkha Rifles were ordered to relieve the two Jak Rif companies in the Cho La area. The two Jak Rif companies were to climb down to Chhanggu, leaving behind a small team of around twenty soldiers manning a post at Cho La. They were to be joined by a team from 7/11 Gorkhas.

So, on 28 September, a platoon of a company (called Charlie or 'C' company[3]) of the Gorkha Rifles battalion along with a medium machine gun (MMG) team, led by Second Lieutenant Samuel, replaced the Jak Rif troops at Point 15180. The other two platoons of that company along with a Signals detachment occupied a location slightly behind Cho La called Twin Huts. A small team of that company was placed at Cho La with an RCL, alongside the team of Jak Rif soldiers.

The higher feature of Point 15450 was supposed to be occupied by another company ('D' or Delta company) of 7/11 Gorkha Rifles led by Lieutenant Ram Singh Rathore. One platoon of that company, along with the mortars, was placed on lower ground behind Point 15450, where the sharp slope of Point 15450 slipped into a natural dugout and provided a crucial vantage position to Indian troops. The Rai Gap provided a concealed space to troops. Positioned away from direct enemy gunfire and observation, the mortars possessed the range and accuracy to reach the Chinese positions across the border.

A day before the 7/11 Gorkha Rifles troops moved to replace the Jak Rif positions, a minor scuffle took place at the border involving the soldiers of Jak Rif and the PLA[4] at Point 15450 at Cho La. On a narrow crest along the border, a little ahead of the Indian sentry post, stood a boulder. For quite some time, the little boulder – about 30 inches high – had been a trivial but testy bone of contention between the soldiers of India and China. The context of the dispute was the disagreement on where the border actually lay. Indian and Chinese forward posts at Point 15450 were situated on either side of the little rock: the two opposing sentry posts of Point 15450 and the rival Chinese post were barely 10 to 12 feet away from each other. According to India's version based on the watershed principle, the boulder on the watershed or the ridgeline marked the boundary. The Chinese believed otherwise and felt the boulder was in their land. Senior Indian officers visiting the post repeatedly urged soldiers to assert the watershed narrative and not give in easily to Chinese threats. It wasn't a surprise then that just over two weeks after the gruesome battle at Nathu La where hundreds of soldiers perished, this boulder became the flashpoint of disagreement at the Cho La pass.

Three Indian soldiers from the Jak Rif battalion got into an argument with a couple of PLA soldiers over the boulder. No side was ready to back down and soon the argument turned into a rough bout of pushing and shoving. Fists and kicks followed and before long it appeared like an ill-tempered football match where the referee had completely lost control. Fortunately, no one opened fire that day.

The next day, the 7/11 Gorkha Rifles battalion troops replaced the Jak Rif troops at that post. Naib Subedar Gyan Bahadur Limbu of the Gorkha battalion, who was reconnoitring the manned sentry post of Point 15450, along with four to five men, had walked up close to the contentious boulder to take in the view on the Chinese side. The sentries at the edge of the Indian and Chinese posts stood at a handshaking distance from each other. Seeing the Indians, about six or seven Chinese soldiers stepped out from their post as well. They stood barely a few feet away from the boulder and looked quite serious. Unaware of the scrap that had taken place the previous day, Gyan Bahadur placed his foot on the boulder. The Chinese soldiers, smarting from the punch-up with the Jak Rif soldiers earlier, suddenly moved menacingly forward and objected aggressively. They were in no mood to relent and a heated argument soon followed.

As the argument was taking place, Ram Singh Rathore, the company commander who was nearby at Point 15450, informed his commanding officer, Lieutenant Colonel K.B. Joshi, that the Chinese were staking claims to the border at the rock, which lay next to the sentry post outside Point 15450. This sentry post, where the scuffle was going on, was visible from the Rai Gap area.[5] KB, who had moved up from a rear location and reached the Rai Gap, noticed a section of Chinese soldiers surround the elevated Point 15450, where the argument was taking place. He let Ram Singh know about the development.[6]

At the disputed rock, Gyan Bahadur placed his foot on the boulder a few times, but each time the Chinese kicked it away. Heated words followed and the Gorkha JCO and five or six armed compatriots from Point 15450, who had accompanied him, came to blows with their Chinese counterparts. One of them unsheathed his bayonet and with a short flick, thrust it into Gyan Bahadur's side.[7] The Gorkha JCO doubled up in pain. Gyan's buddy brought out his khukri and slashed the arm of the Chinese who had bayoneted his senior. Soon, a bunch of Gorkha soldiers emerged from the nearby post of Point 15450, next to the scene of the brawl close to the disputed rock.

The brawl was rapidly growing into a dangerous skirmish. As the Chinese soldiers took up positions at point-blank range, the clanking sounds of rifles being cocked raised fears that a revenge for Nathu La was being unleashed. On either side of the disputed rock, the posts were so close to each other that opening with small arms fire, even rifles, was bound to be fatal. Soon, a volley of Chinese bullets flew at the Indian soldiers who had rushed to the rock. The Chinese hadn't waited for the brawls to prolong for days, as they had done at Nathu La. Instead they had responded quickly, in an attempt to seize an early advantage.

Clearly, the Chinese post commander was prepared to expand the fight and increase the collateral damage. He may have had orders to do so, since the timing of the opening of small arms fire was similar to Nathu La: the Indian soldiers were caught out in the open. Besides, they were aware that the Gorkha soldiers were a temporary replacement for the Jak Rif companies, and hence were not likely to have had a full complement of available ammunition and operational preparation at that location. The Chinese, besides having been located at these posts for a much longer time, had a numerical superiority over their enemy who were temporary occupants at the posts: there were two platoons of around sixty Chinese soldiers of the PLA on the opposite side of India's Point 15450, which had a platoon of around thirty Gorkha soldiers.

As soon as the Chinese started firing, Lance Naik Krishna Bahadur, the section commander, who had been at the rock, took charge and gathered a few more men who had arrived from Point 15450 behind him. They tried to assault the Chinese bunkers a few metres ahead of him across the border. A hail of bullets felled him, though he continued to exhort his men against the Chinese while simultaneously firing at the enemy. A machine gun finally silenced him. Intense fighting had erupted between the two sides by now.

Debi Prasad, who had been present at the scene of the brawl, had been fighting alongside Krishna Bahadur all this while. He now waded into Chinese territory, attacking PLA soldiers who were out in the open and then barged his way past them towards the Chinese forward post, barely a few feet away, across the border. Affable, gentle and jovial, young Limbu from the hills of Nepal rushed into a fierce close-quarter combat with the Chinese at the post. Letting out the war cry 'Jai Maa Kali, Ayo Gorkhali', the young Gorkha thrust towards the well-armed Chinese soldiers. In a flash, he drew out the deadly khukri, raised it to the sky and brough it down on the Chinese light machine gunner before his forefinger could pull the trigger.

Debi moved like lightning as he swiped, swung and slashed, letting the traditional shiny dagger heave and strike in a fearsome display of hand-to-hand combat. He scythed through the Chinese forward line of defence, lopping off five heads as soldiers fell around him. The collective might of the enemy front line was not enough to stop this short, sturdy young man. By the time a desperate bullet knocked him dead, Debi Prasad had

11 Gorkha Rifles Centre

Cho La hero Debi Prasad Limbu.

dismantled the Chinese defensive wall at their post across the border opposite Point 15450. He died inside Chinese territory.

On the Indian side, at Point 15450, Ram Singh Rathore sustained injuries on his left arm as the Chinese kept firing. Unable to use his arm, he kept encouraging his men till a volley of bullets split open his abdomen. After Ram Singh died, Point 15450 was left without an officer, as the Chinese continued to charge forward.

As the Chinese advanced towards Point 15450, they brought down heavy fire on areas close to the Rai Gap (which was nestled in the slope behind Point 15450). The firing incapacitated the mobile fire controller at the Rai Gap as a round pierced his thigh. The mortar gun was thus left unattended. Kul Bhushan, who was close to him, took over the mortar and rained bombs on Chinese soldiers who had closed in towards Point 15450 by then. The impact was sudden and the Chinese advance was held back by the dropping of mortar bombs. The Chinese were not about to give up. A route to Point 15450 existed from a cliff behind it. As a Chinese column tried to scale it, Kul Bhushan noticed some movement and took aim. He fired at them intermittently, killing a few of the climbers.[8] That stopped further movement up the cliff.

The Indian side nonetheless suffered heavy casualties at the lower Rai Gap area but Chinese attempts to overrun the post were thwarted by an effective MMG mounted atop the nearby height of 15180, from where the Gorkhas rained continuous fire. Repeated Chinese attempts failed to capture the gap between the two dominating features of Point 15450 and Point 15180 since the doughty Jak Rif troops at Cho La presented stiff resistance along with the Gorkhas.

Though attacks on the Cho La pass and the Rai Gap, the two low-lying Indian posts, hadn't succeeded, the Chinese kept pounding these positions. The Chinese had earlier successfully downed the Indians at Point 15450 and were now able to dominate Rai Gap with their HMGs that they had positioned in their post opposite Cho La. Knowing that K.B. Joshi had been in the bunker at Rai Gap a short while ago, the Chinese blew up the structure. KB's aggressive retaliation with mortars had drawn Chinese attention to that area and they came down heavy with unrelenting fire. As KB emerged from the demolished bunker, amid smoke and dust, the waiting Chinese snipers, who were in Indian territory now, took aim and fired. Recovering his senses quickly, he took cover just in the nick of time. KB nudged his compatriot next to him. But his buddy was dead, shot by the sniper.

When there was a momentary lull in Chinese firing, KB, the lion-hearted infantry veteran, decided to take over. Preserving his cover, he leaned over and saw the Chinese snipers at a distance – they looked self-assured and a little overconfident. His rifle had got lost while he was escaping the fire earlier but he noticed his dead buddy's rifle next to him, slung over his shoulder. KB snatched it out of the dead man's grasp and aimed through the aperture as his forefinger curled around the trigger.[9] A moment later, the first Chinese sniper slumped dead. He fired again, and this time he brought down the second sniper.

The Chinese HMG firing was continuing to dominate the lower Indian areas of the Rai Gap and the post at

Cho La, demolishing the bunkers and features at will. Narayan Parulekar, the young adjutant of 7/11 Gorkha Rifles whom we met in chapter four, was trying to crawl from the Twin Huts to join the battling Gorkha troops and the small complement of Jak Rif soldiers at Cho La. Paru, as he was known, was a doughty, tenacious soldier who would never give up, but had been pinned down due to heavy strafing.

At this point, it was a man from the village of Lamahatta near Darjeeling, Havildar Tinjong, who stepped forward to change the course of the battle. Tinjong, as we know, had recently returned from a course on RCL guns at the Military School in Mhow (Madhya Pradesh). Tinjong's deft handling of the weapon came in for praise from his instructor at Mhow. The instructor noticed how, even with increasing difficulty levels, young Tinjong remained calm and focused. A feisty fellow from the hills of upper Darjeeling, gifted with razor-sharp reflexes and a strong upper body, Tinjong was waiting with his favourite heavy gun at Cho La. It was time to put to use his learnings from Mhow.

Despite the fog and confusion of the battle, the young havildar had smartly figured out that the HMG on the Chinese side opposite the Indian forward post of Point 15450 that had caused maximum devastation on the Indian side needed to be neutralized. He knew that his RCL had the best chance of taking on the Chinese HMG that was causing havoc. Tinjong silenced the heavy machine gun with his RCL, blasting out the machine gun detachment that was causing trouble. A loud volley aimed at the machine gun team took them out in a flash of smoke. Tinjong, on his part, kept up the fire till his ammunition was exhausted. His barrage of shelling had come as an unexpected turn for the Chinese. He had taken away the advantage from the Chinese in a matter of minutes.

Using the respite created by Tinjong, Paru joined his men at the Cho La post and they used their MMG to

11 Gorkha Rifles Centre

Havildar Tinjong Lama, who used his RCL gun to blast the Chinese bunkers and changed the course of the battle at Cho La.

target the Chinese bunkers opposite Cho La. Despite the heavy volume of fire from both sides, the Chinese did not use artillery fire.[10] Artillery shelling, which is more devastating and has a longer range of fire than either HMGs or RCLs, could have inflicted more damage to the Indian posts but both sides used machine guns and mortars. After an incessant, furious exchange of fire for a few hours, the Chinese abruptly stopped firing and sent up a very light flare – a form of battlefield illumination that provides light in the sky without explosion and can be noticed from a distance – indicating their desire to call a truce, but the Indians continued to rain fire to which the Chinese retaliated occasionally. After a while firing from both sides came to a stop.

The soldiers on both sides were scattered in different parts of the watershed from where they had been taking cover and firing, if they hadn't been blown up entirely. Kul Bhushan, last seen at the Rai Gap, was missing and Narayan Paruleker had spent considerable time trying to locate the commanding officer of his battalion. The sun was setting and there was no sign of Kul Bhushan.[11] Was he lost? Injured? Dead? Paru returned form Cho La to the Twin Huts area behind Cho La, looking for him. When he entered a bunker in the Twin Huts area and found KB hastily reporting the incident on the phone to his boss, the brigade commander, he sighed with relief.

'At least I have one officer with me, sir,' stammered the overjoyed KB upon seeing his young officer. The reality soon dawned on everyone that many of the Indian soldiers on 15450 had perished and that the post had been captured by the advancing Chinese.

Kul Bhushan kept insisting with the brigade commander on the phone that he be allowed a chance that same night to launch a counterattack to retake the post.[12] He had encountered intermittent firing from the post, indicating the Chinese intention to dominate from the captured post. He knew that delaying the counterattack by more than a day would allow the Chinese to bring in reinforcements. He assessed there were a few likely surviving Chinese soldiers on Point 15450 and wanted a quick counterattack. The brigade commander and Kul Bhushan agreed on the need for the cover of darkness to launch the assault. The two officers now awaited the arrival of reinforcements to accompany them. But in the muddle and confusion the artillery detachment, which had been called in hastily to provide support for the counterattack, arrived without its operators.[13]

KB had spent enough time in the area, and having been there a few years ago to build the Cho La post, knew the terrain well. The attacking column chose an area for a buildup that was not known to everyone. It was the steeper side to the Point 15450 feature and was called Black Rocks because of the rocky terrain. KB, along with Paru, led the attacking column into the area. Black Rocks proved to be a rough climb and the column was stumbling over the rocks.[14] Soon enough, the attacking party was caught out by the glare of magnesium flares[15] that had been shot into the sky by the Chinese at Post 15450 to identify the moving figures at Black Rocks. The Chinese knew the approach and lay in wait for the Indian attackers.

Changing tactics, KB and Narayan formed two teams and each took a different approach. KB led the frontal attack as Narayan moved in from the side.[16] The few Chinese who had survived the battle and stayed on top of the feature had sensed the build-up against them. Their reinforcements hadn't arrived yet and now they were up against a determined Indian counterattacking force. This was going to be a massacre, they soon realized.

When KB and Narayan arrived at the top of the feature, the Chinese had already fled. Taking a tactically smart decision, they had chosen to evade a mismatched battle against a larger force, and escaped from the post.[17] Kul Bhushan's decision to launch the counterattack the same evening had saved the territory from slipping into Chinese hands. He and his men stood tall in the darkness, having taken back the lost land. The Indians had recaptured Point 15450 from the Chinese.

It was a dark night when the madness ended, but the silence of death in every cranny and on every slope was nauseating. KB and his men found the body of Ram Singh Rathore at Point 15450. Apparently, the PLA had tried to drag him over to the Chinese side but fled hurriedly as the Indians approached the top.[18] The post was littered with bodies, limbs and torsos.

Debi Prasad Limbu and others who charged in an assault earlier had perished on Chinese territory while a few of those Chinese soldiers who launched an attack on the Indian post lay dead next to it, having crossed the border. There were those who had died in their bunkers, blown to bits by the shelling and heavy fire. The Chinese post, with its HMG, opposite Cho La lay demolished by Tinjong's accurate firing and the relentless firing by the Jak Rif soldiers at Cho La. A couple of Chinese had plunged to their deaths at the foot of Point 15450, while a Gorkha jawan lay crushed under a rock and another one had died holding the insides of his stomach that had been ripped open. Then there were those poor souls who lay alone, unattended, life slowly ebbing away. Soon, 'martyrdom' would be celebrated briefly on both sides of the border and beautiful citations would be written on the deaths of the soldiers. Over time though, the lives lost in these lonely, barren corners would end up as unnoticed footnotes in history.

~

A couple of days later, the bodies were exchanged. The Chinese had dragged some of the bodies from the Indian post of Point 15450 over to their side. A few Indians, such as Debi Prasad, had died on the Chinese side. One of the Indian army officers at the exchange ceremony was taken aside by the Chinese commander and asked about Debi Prasad. They had watched him tear through the Chinese forward post's defensive screen with his khukri. Soldiers on the Indian side recall the Chinese calling him the Tiger of Chola.[19] His bravery had left a deep impact. 'Who the hell was he?' the Chinese officer asked his Indian counterpart, assigned to recover the bodies, clearly awestruck at Debi's courage.

Debi Prasad and the other Indian soldiers had not died in vain. They had succeeded in not ceding even an inch to the Chinese at Cho La and Nathu La. Their bravery had made one thing clear: it was now difficult to breach Indian defences through the Sikkim sector. The vulnerable Siliguri Corridor at the foot of the Sikkim hills suddenly seemed unreachable and far to the Chinese.

Many PLA soldiers had died in the two battles – with

340 having been killed at Nathu La and thirty to thirty-five at Cho La. Many Indian soldiers too lost their lives, about eighty-eight at Nathu La and around fifteen at Cho La. The setback at Cho La, especially the deadly close combat skills of Debi and Krishna, had resulted in pushing back the Chinese post almost three kilometres inside their territory at a place called Kham barracks[20] and away from encountering khukri-wielding Gorkhas at close range. India had managed to overcome China at Nathu La and Cho La, a small but critical redemption that exorcized the ghosts of 1962. The two battles didn't result in the gain of any territory. Both sides went back to where they had been before the conflict began. But these battles would turn out to be a watershed in the region's history, events that heralded an era of peace between India and China. By showing China that India was no pushover, and that the Indian army would defend India's borders, these battles ironically were harbingers of peace. By showing China that the Sikkim sector couldn't be breached to link up with East Pakistani forces at the other end of the Siliguri Corridor, the Indian army had made sure that Peking would never embark on such a misadventure. For China, psychological warfare was a crucial way to dominate an entire army's strategic mindspace. Nathu La and Cho La would become the

inflection points of the turnaround in psychological ascendancy. Nathu La and Cho La had set the template for the next half a century and more.

However, in 1967, though the Indian army had performed well and got the better of China in the two battles, the loss of around a hundred lives at Nathu La and Cho La was not acceptable. The prime minister had to face a barrage of criticism in Parliament from the opposition leader Piloo Mody. After the battles, Sagat was posted out to Mizoram, in what was considered a blow to his career prospects. This even though he had successfully led India in the bloodiest battles since the 1962 war with China, and come out more successful than his predecessors. Sagat's actions did not go down too well with a section of the leadership in Delhi.

However, his foresight, the strategic implications and damage to the nation's geographic fabric arising from a tactical withdrawal from the border in Sikkim and his stubbornness to stand by his decision were boons for India in the long run.

History would go on to judge Sagat Singh more generously than his contemporaries did.

After the storm of Cho La there prevailed an uneasy calm in Sikkim. In the rest of the time the 7th Battalion spent there, no scuffles or quarrels occurred. In fact,

Captain Paru would occasionally end up making small talk with the Chinese interpreter across the border. Life along the border had calmed down and neither the Chinese nor the Indians chose to escalate any further issues.

~

Along the border there lay several minefields. Soldiers had to be careful while setting out on patrols in the area. Once the soldiers found a yak calf stuck inside a minefield – alive and lucky not to have stepped on one of the mines placed underneath the ground. The Gorkha soldiers, plainly ferocious in their attack on the Chinese barely a month ago, decided to crawl through the minefield, picking the safe lanes in it, risking their lives to rescue the poor animal that was struggling for life. The calf was eventually rescued and brought to the battalion, where he became a favourite of the soldiers. They gave him a name – Somnath – and adopted him as the battalion mascot. Soon Somnath was made a 'lance naik' and given the stripe associated with the rank. Lance Naik Somnath would visit all pickets and posts and attend all parades and functions. Somnath quickly made his way through the ranks to become a lance havildar.[21]

Six months after the Cho La battle, news arrived of the battalion's move from Sikkim. K.B. Joshi led his unit out of the location to Dehradun, having endured the worst part of the winter. The news of going to Dehradun was greeted with loud cheers by the boys – but there was a tinge of unhappiness. They had been told that Somnath wouldn't survive the heat of Dehradun and that he would need to stay back in Sikkim. With a heavy heart, the battalion handed over Lance Havildar Somnath to the zoo in Darjeeling before they left for Dehradun.

The other victorious battalions would also soon leave Sikkim for their next locations. The 2nd Grenadiers had attained glory at Nathu La. Rai Singh was awarded the Mahavir Chakra for gallantry while Captain Dagar's charge was rewarded with a Vir Chakra. Major Harbhajan from 18 Rajput, who had accompanied him on that attack, was awarded the Vir Chakra as well.

Amongst the Cho La warriors, Debi Prasad Limbu would be awarded a Vir Chakra – India's third highest gallantry medal in war – for an action that deserved a greater honour.[22] Tinjong, who had blasted out the Chinese with his RCL, would return to Mhow as an instructor to train others with the weapon – instilling in them the virtues of keeping a still, unflappable head in a tough situation. In Mhow, he would receive the news that he was being awarded the Vir Chakra.

What of Kul Bhushan Joshi? KB's recapture of the Cho La post would remain the last action of battle between India and China. Fifty years later, KB would still remain the last victor in a battle between the two arch-rivals.

Part 3

Epilogue

After the Watershed Battles

News of victories at Nathu La and Cho La flickered briefly on the front pages of mainstream Indian newspapers in 1967 but soon became mere passing mentions in the media. Over time, they would be forgotten. After the battles, a deflated Peking tacitly cooperated with New Delhi to hush up the news.[1] But why did Delhi choose to downplay the battles? Perhaps because the battles of 1967 were too closely tied to memories of the horrific defeat of 1962. Highlighting the victories of 1967 could bring into focus and remind people once again of the military indecisiveness and political ineptness displayed in 1962. Perhaps also because India soon got a blockbuster military moment to celebrate in the form of the 1971 victory against Pakistan. And so Rai Singh and his brave Grenadiers were forgotten and Kul Bhushan Joshi faded into oblivion, unrecognized as the

181

victors of the battle of Cho La. Sagat was sent to the woods of northeast India with a mandate to set right a rapidly growing insurgency in Mizoram, where he again led a successful campaign – the first such victory against insurgent rebels in India. He took centrestage and won the 1971 war for India four years later. It was due entirely to these commanders and their men that the sun set forever on battles between India and China. The battles of 1967 were also an important and unrecognized determinant in India's spectacular victory against Pakistan in 1971. It is to this story, full of international intrigue, that we now turn.

~

Two years had passed since India and China battled each other at Cho La and Nathu La. Then, on Saturday, 3 May 1969, opportunity presented itself on a solemn occasion. It was the funeral of Indian president Zakir Husain who had died in office.[2] There were many foreign attendees at his funeral in Delhi, but a surprise guest showed up in the form of the Chinese charge d'affaires. The Chinese dignitary's presence was unusual as there had been no diplomatic relations between India and China since 1962. But that day marked a change. There was a little backstory behind that initiative, one involving that nemesis of China, Indira Gandhi. 'Yingdila Gandi', as the Chinese called her, was often lampooned in the Chinese media, with slogans such as 'Yingdila Meikdila', which on translation meant 'Indira influenced by American imperialism'.[3]

Earlier, on New Year's Eve in 1968, when Prime Minister Indira Gandhi had taken an initiative to broker peace, the Chinese had flatly turned down the offer. The feisty premier, not used to being rebuffed, persisted with her move, even reiterating at a public rally that 'if the US and China could have rapport even after the Vietnam war and the Cultural Revolution, why wouldn't India follow a similar policy?'

But in spite of the Indian prime minister's overtures, disagreements and bitter acrimony cropped up every now and then. In late April 1969, Brajesh Mishra, then a senior Indian diplomat in Peking (and later India's national security adviser), walked out of a reception accorded by Zhou Enlai in honour of Air Marshal Nur Khan, a senior leader of the Pakistan government, to protest a Chinese remark about supporting the people of Jammu and Kashmir in their 'struggle for self-determination'.[4] China responded by boycotting the centenary birth celebrations of Mahatma Gandhi that year.[5] China also upped the ante by issuing India a démarche in April to remove troops from Nathu La.[6] India chose not to respond this time and the Chinese decided not to pursue the démarche any further.

So the Chinese charge d'affairs showing up at President Zakir Husain's funeral was not only unexpected, but it also significantly calmed the bilateral relationship. The shadow of peace was beginning to extend. In June 1969, when Indira Gandhi was visiting Kabul, the Chinese charge d'affaires attended the reception held in her honour. When Naga insurgent leaders arrived in China later that year, they weren't provided the assistance they sought and instead left empty-handed. Their leader confessed, 'Chinese support to militant groups in India was being reassessed.'[7] By that time, the Chinese had also withdrawn support for the Naxals.

In fact, China ceased to view India as an entity that could be overrun. Scholars were of the view that the degree to which the Sino-India military equation had changed from the time of the 1962 Chinese invasion was manifest in September 1967.[8] Whilst India might never be in a position to pose a military threat to its neighbour, it now possessed the capability of repelling Chinese aggression deftly and damaging its reputation.

But the exchanges between India and China were still far from warm and China had a tendency of blowing hot and cold. Added to this mix was the trouble brewing in East Pakistan, which would give the Chinese an opportunity to get back at India. The Soviet premier, Alexei Kosygin, opined that Chinese foreign policy was an unpredictable entity because 'Mao was a completely unbalanced person and one must be ready to expect him to behave in an unpredictable manner'.

Kosygin's remarks are likely due to the tetchy relationship between China and the USSR in the late 1960s, something that could have impacted India–China relations. Mao had been deeply concerned about the designs of the more powerful communist nation, which had conquered the Czech Republic the previous year. The Brezhnev doctrine, which declared that the Soviet Union could intervene in any fraternal country deviating from the socialist track, often made Mao feel insecure.[9]

China for its part was still spiralling due to the cultural revolution. During the period of the revolution around 1968, foreign embassies and consulates in China were targeted. The Vietnamese consulate in Kunming was attacked, while Japanese correspondents were deported on frivolous grounds. Finding no resistance, the Chinese revolutionaries then turned on the Soviets and their embassy in China was attacked. An officer of a Russian ship anchored in Dairen Harbour was paraded through the streets for refusing to wear a badge with Mao Zedong's photo on it.[10] Border talks between the two nations also turned out to be a dismal failure.[11]

The Soviets were gradually building up a response to their fellow belligerent communist nation. By 1969,[12] US intelligence detected Russian preparations for attacks on China's nuclear facilities. Soviet ICBMs threatened key locations in China as Peking didn't possess such sophisticated weapons.[13] Sparring was bound to happen at some point.

The focal point of the eruption would be Zhenbao Island, a dot of land on the Ussuri river north of Vladivostok under the control of the Soviet Union and along the border with China. The Soviets got a dose of just how unpredictable Mao could be when a Chinese patrol consisting of three platoons, supported by an artillery unit, confronted a regular Soviet squad of seven guards and killed them.

The incident led to a fierce gun battle between the two nations. The Soviets launched a blistering counterattack with tanks, artillery and armed personnel carriers. The Russians steamrolled the Chinese and dealt a humiliating defeat to Mao. American satellite pictures that captured the surface of Zhenbao Island showed how the Chinese side of Ussuri 'was so pockmarked by Soviet artillery that it looked like a moonscape'.[14]

After the Zhenbao Island episode, the Soviets focused on amassing a powerful build-up along the border, which involved forty-eight military divisions! Russian minister Marshal Greschko told an Indian envoy that the forces were 'five to seven times more than before'. This essentially tied the Chinese down to their northern border in a major way.

It wasn't just the USSR that China was on frosty terms with. China had undergone a period of isolation during Mao's Cultural Revolution from 1966 onwards, which resulted in the freezing of relations with other countries, and the only ones that remained China's friends were Pakistan and Albania. Internationally, Mao and China were boxed into an isolated corner.[15] It was in the light of such developments that the Chinese overtures to India around 1969 were significant.

The US had been watching the exchanges involving China and the Soviets and sensed an opportunity to create a stronger front against its arch-rival superpower, the USSR. A new republican government had been elected in the US, with Richard Nixon as the new occupant of the White House. Henry Kissinger, the clever and canny foreign secretary of Nixon, initiated the move to befriend China, trusting the time-tested adage that 'your enemy's enemy is your friend'.

Nixon and Kissinger believed that building relations

with China would isolate the Soviets and were exploring a conduit to connect with the Chinese. Henry Kissinger secretly flew to China to meet Zhou Enlai in 1971 and was instantly awestruck by the Chinese premier.[16] Zhou gave him a book on the India–China 1962 war, written by an Australian journalist, Neville Maxwell, that was critical of India and praised China.[17] Subsequently, the book made a profound impact in shaping Kissinger's opinion on India and helped him guide Nixon's inner bias on foreign policy choices in the subcontinent. Nixon agreed with his minister's assessment: 'Great guys these Chinese are', Nixon would later tell Kissinger, post a meeting with Zhou Enlai.

Meanwhile, trouble was brewing in China's closest ally, Pakistan. Elections in 1970 resulted in a rude shock for dominant political parties in West Pakistan. A party from East Pakistan – consisting largely of a population that spoke Bangla instead of Urdu – had won. Sheikh Mujibur Rahman[18] of the Awami League now staked a claim to be prime minister.

For decades, the Bengali population had felt marginalized by the richer, powerful Punjabi–Pathan elite. As the people of East Pakistan finally found their voice through the ballot box and hoped to be represented in Parliament and form government, a clampdown by the West Pakistani establishment brought to life their worst fears: West Pakistan began to treat them as a lesser colony. A subsequent people's uprising in East Pakistan was put down ruthlessly by Yahya Khan and his army in on of the worst massacres since the Second World War.[19]

For Nixon and Kissinger,[20] this didn't matter. Pakistan, Peking's closest ally, was a conduit for establishing relations with China and it may not have served American interests to criticize Pakistan at that stage.

President Nixon and his foreign secretary Kissinger believed they were on the brink of making history with China and that this would overshadow their decision to support Pakistan, tainted as it was with the deaths of a million people in Bangladesh. Refugees began to flood into India, searching for shelter and safety in India's northeast and eastern states.[21] Prime Minister Indira Gandhi would decisively move towards aiding the local resistance movement in East Pakistan called the Mukti Bahini. Indira believed that the refugee exodus would overwhelm India and wanted to send the Indian army into Bangladesh to help the Mukti Bahini. Besides, this was her chance to split Pakistan and neutralize the threat of having a hostile neighbour to both the country's east and west.

In May 1971, Indira Gandhi called a cabinet meeting of ministers and service chiefs where she announced her intent. But chief of army staff, General Sam Manekshaw said, 'Madam, if we were to go in now, the monsoons are underway and my forces wouldn't be able to cross the rivers that are flooded. We would lose the war.' Manekshaw argued that there were better chances of a victory if he was given six more months. He resisted the plan to attack in haste and threatened to resign if she went ahead with it.[22] Indira Gandhi, despite her authoritarian nature, preferred to let the army operate independently[23] and gave in. The prime minister had developed a quiet belief in her army chief, who had been her personal pick[24] over the other strong contender for chief, Lieutenant General Harbaksh Singh, the hero of 1965.

Nixon and Kissinger meanwhile thought that supporting Pakistan would not only be a convenient way of getting closer to China but also that it would serve as a warning because India had gotten closer to the Soviets during this time. Besides Nixon, who called Indira Gandhi a 'bitch', and Kissinger, who called Indians 'bastards', were also animated by a profound anti-Indian sentiment. When L.K. Jha, Indian ambassador to the US, told Kissinger that India might send back some of the refugees from East Pakistan as guerrillas, Nixon commented, 'By God we will cut off economic aid.'[25] India had found itself vulnerable to the possibility of having to square up against a formidable alliance of Pakistan, China and the US. Indira Gandhi signed an Indo-Soviet

Treaty of Peace, Friendship and Cooperation that forbade both countries from 'providing any assistance to any third party that engages in conflict with the other party'. Indira subsequently also got assurances from the Soviets of aid in the event of an armed conflict. The treaty and promise of aid placed the Soviets and the Americans in rival camps in South Asia.

Kissinger believed that the entry of the Soviets into the mix would push the Chinese – so far non-committal – into being an active part of the alliance against India. He was now coaxing China to move troops to the Indian border. According to the chairman of joint chiefs of staff at the White House, this would mean India would have to divert five or six divisions to the Chinese border.[26] That would have created a situation similar to 1965, when India had to commit troops at the Chinese border near Sikkim, thereby scuttling its thrust against Pakistan.

The Americans were keen for the Chinese to pressurize and scare India. But Peking decided not to move large numbers of troops towards the Indian border. There were a few critical reasons for this, including the huge internal turmoil in the country and the belligerent Soviets to its north. But perhaps the most important reason for China not entering the war, one that is grossly underplayed, was India's strong defence of the Sikkim watershed in 1965 and 1967 which made it more difficult for China to block the Siliguri Corridor to aid Pakistan. The importance of the fact that China did not enter the war due to India's outstanding defence of the Sikkim sector in those years cannot be overstated. Indeed, it made a critical difference to the outcome of the 1971 war.

Way back, in December 1965, as the focus shifted towards the post-1965 peace agreement that was to take place in Tashkent, an important decision was taken in an obscure corner of the Himalayas that would save India from disaster in 1971. The singular decision of Lieutenant General Sagat Singh to dig in at Nathu La and guard the watershed, despite the immense pressure he faced to withdraw, helped India stay at the heights on the watershed and protect the Siliguri Corridor and the rest of India – both in 1967 and, importantly, again in 1971.

If the watershed line and Nathu La had not been occupied by India, Chinese forces would have found it easier to attack from the heights, roll down towards Sikkim in 1971 and sweep through Indian defences on lower ground, linking up with waiting Pakistani troops on the other side of the Siliguri Corridor – barely 25 kilometres at its broadest – in Bangladesh.[27] A hammer-and-anvil movement, the kind China envisaged would have presented itself on a platter. The Siliguri Corridor could have been split in quick time by a rampaging PLA. And they would have been able to do this without diverting significant troops from their border with the USSR.

Were this hammer-and-anvil movement not to have taken place, had Nathu La been vacated in 1965 and China occupied it, then even mere posturing by the Chinese during the 1971 war could have majorly influenced India's plans in Bangladesh. But China could not manage to pressurize India at the Sikkim border after the setback in 1967 – all thanks to Sagat and his brave men. The lessons from Nathu La and Cho La had also put the burden of psychological doubt on the Chinese.

By November 1971 the monsoon had receded. It was a little over six months since Sam Manekshaw had famously said in a cabinet meeting that he needed time for the army to wage a winnable war. The bugle of war was finally sounded on 3 December 1971. As night broke, sirens screamed overhead, airplanes took off from bases, and a fierce air battle opened the war. Pakistan knew the overwhelming strength of the Indian army in the eastern wing was difficult to match. Bhutto once again decided to beg the Chinese for support to deter India.

But the Chinese held firm that they did not want to play an active role in the war by diverting Indian defence commitments, like they had done earlier in 1965. Instead, they wanted Pakistan to handle the conflict on its own.

Nixon and Kissinger, ever optimistic, continued to do their best to coax China to scare the Indians. Nixon believed that Indians were 'cowards'[28] who would be scared by any sort of movement by China and kept persuading the Chinese to do something. 'All they have to do is move something. Move some trucks, fly some planes,' stated Nixon. Finally, when the Chinese began to move skeletal troops to the Sikkim border, it was a far cry from the aggressive posture of 1965. Unlike in 1965, there was no ultimatum issued by China this time. Pushed to a corner, the Americans desperately resorted to a final throw of the dice. On 10 December 1971, a posse of cars with security personnel arrived at a nondescript CIA safehouse in New York's Upper East Side that had no doorman. At the unusual location, Henry Kissinger[29] had come to meet Huang Hua, the Chinese ambassador to the UN. Kissinger virtually extended to China an open invitation to attack India. He let Huang know that the US was sending a fleet of destroyers and aircraft carriers to the Indian Ocean to weaken India's ability to defend itself.[30] Aware of China's wariness about Soviet interference, Kissinger promised help: 'The US would oppose efforts of others to interfere with the People's Republic.' Kissinger was now confident that China would finally move its troops against India. He was wrong, again.

The dragon had lost its fire. Although the Chinese

resorted to the usual diatribe against India, the Indian embassy in Peking noted that the *People's Daily* refrained from mentioning direct action.[31] China would raise feeble protests about seven Indian troops who had crossed the Sikkim border and a few PLA troops even marched towards the border. But India wasn't much bothered about these threats.[32] Zhou's anti-India tirade in a speech in Peking was a cosmetic show of support to Pakistan that Indian diplomats who attended laughed off as 'impotent rage'.[33]

The war ended before the US could meaningfully intervene. Swift and brutal, it lasted fourteen days. John Mearsheimer called it India's blitzkrieg.[34] In two weeks, the Indian army, with six divisions under the astute and perceptive battlefield commander Sagat Singh crossed the Meghna river and headed straight for Dacca. In an unprecedented move, he used heliborne operations to lift an entire infantry brigade across the mighty river Meghna. This action surprised the Pakistani defenders, who hadn't expected the troops to cross the Meghna river. Sagat believed that the capture of Dacca was essential for winning the war.[35] It was a throwback to the elements of surprise and decisiveness he had employed at Nathu La in 1967 – of taking initiative to use artillery to stun the Chinese.[36]

After Dacca fell, Pakistan surrendered on 16 December. An elaborate surrender ceremony followed signifying the

Colonel Ranvijay Singh

Sagat Singh discussing plans for the capture of
Dhaka during the 1971 India–Pakistan war.

first comprehensive victory in war since the Second World
War. It was a victory on several counts. Bangladesh was
born out of a nation that prided itself on the two-nation
theory: it was a victory of secular forces over communal
forces who had massacred their own people.

Despite the desperate efforts of the American
leadership, the war remained confined to the neighbouring
adversaries and did not escalate into a larger conflict. This
was the most important result of the 1967 battles of Cho
La and Nathu La.

~

After the surrender ceremony, 1971. Sam Manekshaw
addressing the troops. Sagat is standing behind him.

After the war, the focus shifted to Sikkim. In October
1972, Sir Terence Garvey, the British high commissioner
in Delhi, visited Sikkim. On arrival at Gangtok, he was
taken to Nathu La by his Indian host. Garvey, in his
report to London upon his return, would make a pertinent
observation about Sikkim. Given that China had invaded
and occupied Tibet, there was a likelihood that it would
do the same in Sikkim to create a buffer with India that
brought it closer to the latter's Gangetic plains. Noting

that 'Sikkim today is more than a geographical expression and the causes are mainly accidental', Garvey added in his report that 'it would be much tidier if Sikkim became a part of India'.[37]

With Pakistan's disappearance on the eastern border, the only option that remained for China in its strategic calculus was for Sikkim to move out of India's political orbit permanently. China as we know had always been interested in the Siliguri Corridor.

Earlier that year, Sagat visited his old friends – the Chogyal and Gyalmo – and stayed at the royal palace. The cheerful evenings of the past returned briefly. One morning, after a late evening of card games and conversations the previous day, the Chogyal chose to surprise the general. Dressed in his avatar as an honorary Indian army officer, the Chogyal led a marching music band of bagpipers and drummers of Sikkim Guards,[38] that played under the window of the palace guest room where Sagat slept. An embarrassed and disconcerted Captain Randhir Sinh, the general's military aide, rushed to the Chogyal, pleading him to stop.[39] The Chogyal was in no mood to relent and played on till Sagat, adequately entertained and visibly amused, arrived at the balcony in his morning robe and acknowledged the gesture with a broad smile and an exaggerated bow.[40] While the Chogyal enjoyed a warm relationship with Sagat and Manekshaw, his relations with other army officers and government officials were not quite the same.

The political officer appointed in Sikkim by the government in Delhi had been at loggerheads with the Chogyal. Hope Cooke's relentless advocacy of autonomy for Sikkim had drawn hostile opposition from political and media quarters in India.[41] The opposition had dubbed her an American spy, though she was unlikely to have been one.

Certain other incidents also ended in distancing the royals from the Indian government. In November 1971, as the gathering war clouds forced Indira Gandhi to fly off to meet Nixon in the US, and the whole of India was in shock over the brutal repression taking place in East Pakistan, Thondup and Hope decided to have a fashion show partnering with one of the finest department stores of New York, Bergdorf Goodman on the plush Fifth Avenue.

On the night of the opening of the show, Sikkimese flags lined both sides of Fifth Avenue and shops were filled with Sikkimese craftwork, flags and souvenirs. Several shows were held, including one at the Smithsonian Hall that ran to a packed house.[42] Reports began to appear in the US newspapers about the travails of a fragile state that was in need of support. The ill-considered timing of the fashion show and the accompanying reports didn't go down well with Indira. In fact, she was annoyed when told about the media coverage of the fashion show in the middle of the growing crisis next to India and Sikkim's borders.[43]

The Research and Analysis Wing, commonly referred as R&AW or RAW, formed in 1968, was a specialized intelligence force. RAW had set up intelligence cells inside Bangladesh that ultimately helped the advancing Indian army with vital intelligence on the Pakistani army and their moles and networks.[44] RAW, under its legendary spymaster R.N. Kao, acquired a halo of credibility as a serious intelligence outfit. After the war, they identified the Siliguri Corridor as the most vulnerable piece of land on the map of India. The creation of Bangladesh had reduced the chances of China linking up with a country to the east of the Siliguri Corridor, since the Bangladesh government and its premier Mujibur Rahman were allies of India. But the task of consolidating India's frontiers remained unfinished. RAW would put together a plan to redraw India's map. Some would claim that the prime minister was unaware of the covert plan to merge Sikkim with India.[45] But a RAW operative, G.B.S. Sidhu, a former special secretary of the agency and station chief in the Sikkim capital Gangtok, clarified in his book that the plan, known to the prime minister, began to take shape in 1972. In December 1972 Indira Gandhi called the RAW chief, R.N. Kao, and her principal secretary, P.N. Haksar, and mentioned that 'the Chogyal was being difficult', wanting 'full sovereign rights'. She asked 'if something could be done about' it. The 'operation' to change the map of Sikkim took shape on the basis of these discussions. In 1973, Sidhu, then a young official with RAW was sent to Gangtok to take charge of the field office.[46]

Towards the close of the 1960s, a popular opposition to the Chogyal had emerged in the form of Kazi Lhendup Dorjee, a leader of the majority Gorkha community in Sikkim.[47] Kazi's movement had gained popularity as the streets of Sikkim swelled with protests against monarchy, supported by the government in Delhi. Soon, Indian government agents began to appear on the streets of Gangtok, socializing with local citizens. The Chogyal, taken aback at reports of meetings involving rebels and government agents,[48] at a meeting with Indira Gandhi at the Himalayan Mountaineering Institute in Gangtok, asked her whether a Naxalite type of rebellion was taking place in Sikkim.[49]

Relations between Indira and Thondup, once warm, were now brittle. Thondup was given short shrift by the prime minister who had little time for him now. He grew cynical about finding an amicable solution for Sikkim. On the personal front, his relationship with Hope had broken down irreconcilably. Around late 1973, Hope finally left for the US along with her children. She never returned to Sikkim and the couple would divorce later in 1980.[50]

RAW was watching the Chogyal's movements. A report came in from London about him going to a Chinese restaurant where he met with Chinese embassy officials.[51] The Indian government had become sensitive towards any news involving ties with the US and China and disapproved of this thoroughly.

B.S. Das, the Indian government's political officer in Sikkim from April 1973 to July 1974, sounded an alarm to the government during his tenure that if India didn't act, China would take advantage of the situation. Indian opinion was coming around to the fact that Nehru's rejection of Patel's idea of integrating Sikkim with the rest of the country had been a blunder that could compromise national security.

In September 1974, the Indian Parliament passed a resolution making Sikkim an associate state of India. Monarchy was retained but the chasm between the palace in Gangtok and the Indian government became unbridgeable. In March 1975, the first signs of the end arrived in the neighbourhood of Nepal. The Chogyal decided to attend the coronation of King Birendra in Nepal, despite Das asking him to refrain from doing so. In Kathmandu, the Chogyal met with Chinese and Pakistani premiers and publicly criticized India on its move regarding Sikkim. This was the final provocation for Indira Gandhi's government.

One fateful morning in April 1975, as Basant Chhettri, a palace guard, strode to his post at the palace gates, from behind a tree outside the gates a rifle took aim at him. Basant noticed a hint of movement and reached for his rifle. As he levelled the muzzle towards the bushes, a few shots were fired from behind the trees. Basant Chhettri dropped dead. A clipped burst of machine-gun fire followed and soon, an attacking column led by a Sikh non-commissioned officer reached the gates and fired at the palace. Basant's eighteen-year-old buddy, Nima Sherpa, stumbled out of the guardroom in surprise and was shot in the arm, which had to be amputated later.[52] The attack was brisk and one-sided.

The Indian army had surrounded the palace and swarmed in within no time. This was a unique moment: the Indian army was fighting the Indian army for the first and only time. Under the provisions of extra regimental employment, the Sikkim Guards had an overall strength of 272 – including 130 Sikkimese soldiers[53] and a few from the Gorkha Rifles. Thus, Indian army soldiers were also a part of the Sikkim Guards, which therefore meant that they were technically defending Sikkim against the Indian state. In an even more awkward twist, the situation also pitted two brothers wearing the same military uniform against each other. Major Harish Jagota, the younger brother from the Jat Regiment, was leading the attacking force of the Indian army that surrounded the palace while the older sibling, Colonel R.K. Jagota, from the Gorkha Regiment, was with Sikkim Guards at that time, defending the Chogyal's forces against the attackers. This was an awkward situation except that no battle would take place that morning and within an hour, soldiers of 17 Division had disarmed the Sikkim Guards who chose not to put up a fight.

The Chogyal was drinking his favourite Rémy Martin when the commandant of the Royal Sikkim Guards, Lieutenant Colonel K.S. Gurung, announced the surrender.[54] Chogyal, an honorary colonel (holding the rank of a major general) of 8 Gorkha Regiment, on hearing that the sentry had been killed, wore his Indian army uniform, walked to the palace gates and saluted the slain soldier.

On 16 May 1975, Sikkim became the twenty-second state of the Indian Union. Palden Thondup would remain a 'royal' albeit without a kingdom.

While the manner in which Sikkim was assimilated by Indira Gandhi's government divided opinions in India,[55] the bigger question was: what would have happened to

Lieutenant Colonel P.C. Saklani

Sikkim Guards carrying out a drill inside palace premises.
Sikkim guards were deployed against the Indian army
sent to take over the palace.

Sikkim had it not become a part of the Indian union?
Garvey had added in his report earlier that he couldn't
see Sikkim's future as an independent entity. Over time
the decision to integrate Sikkim proved to be correct,
given its geopolitical reality and subsequent performance
as one of India's better-run states. In hindsight, it can
be argued that the presence of Sikkim on India's map
gave the country a strategic buffer against China for its
north-eastern states.

In the 1960s, every time tensions between India and
China escalated, apprehensions increased along the
Sikkim border. With Sikkim's integration into India, the

direct threat to the Siliguri Corridor was reduced, though the Chinese still lined up on the opposite side.

When Sikkim was assimilated into India in 1975, India's action evoked strong protests from China and the international community[56] but finally in 2003, both countries agreed to bury their differences on Sikkim and accept the border as a legitimate one between India and China.

~

The positive effects of India's victory in 1967 were not only visible in the 1971 war, but there have been at least two other concrete instances where the salubrious knock-on effects have played an important role. We will now look at each of these in turn.

As mentioned earlier in the book, in October 1966, Chinese soldiers entered the contentious Doklam plateau in Bhutan – a strategic location close to the Jampheri ridge that overlooks the Siliguri Corridor. The acrimonious incident worsened the already fractious relationship between India and China and culminated in the brutal battles of the next year.

In more recent times, specifically in 2017, a PLA platoon discreetly arrived in the Doklam area near the Doklam plateau again.[57] The Doklam plateau is still an unresolved territorial dispute between China and Bhutan, despite twenty-four rounds of talks.[58] The point of contention has been a trijunction where international boundaries of India, China and Bhutan meet. While India and Bhutan consider such an international boundary at the Batangla Pass, China believes that such a point was 89 kilometres further south at Mount Gymochen.[59]

Upon entering the Dolam area, the PLA destroyed the stone bunkers that the Royal Bhutan Army (RBA) had constructed years ago and manned occasionally. As the Chinese track construction party started the survey and alignment work on the plateau, Indian soldiers came down from the nearby Doklam area (the battles at Nathu La and Cho La in 1967 had led to a substantial increase in Indian forces stationed in Bhutan permanently) and prevented the PLA soldiers from pursuing their work. A brief scuffle ensued and the two sides entered into a tense face-off that almost brought the two countries to the edge of a conflict once again. India pursued a limited aim to stop the building of Chinese infrastructure in the area and retained a dogged presence. India's decision to stand by Bhutan in 2017 won the latter's trust. There is no evidence Peking would not move the goalposts of its territorial claim further south if it were able to secure the Doklam plateau.[60]

At the leadership level though, the consequences

this time were different. First, India's riposte, unlike the one fifty years ago, was a stolidly unflappable one, phlegmatic yet firm. In 1966, the premiers had been pulled into the quarrel almost immediately, with Indira Gandhi instinctively stepping up the offensive in her press briefings about China. Five decades later, the responses of both Xi Jinping and Narendra Modi – the two premiers on either side – were low-key, even as the Chinese state media ranted. It was at the military leadership level that the confidence, a legacy of 1967, was manifest. `Complete operational autonomy had been delegated to the commanders on ground and we were geared up for a long haul,' remembered Lieutenant General Pravin Bakshi, who was commanding the Eastern Command at that time. When the confrontation with Chinese troops at Doklam started earlier that year, a brigade commander, accompanied by his sahayak walked across and warned Chinese troops to move back. Indian troops formed human chains and refused to back down.[61]

The two countries ultimately managed to dial down the aggression after a prolonged disagreement that brought them perilously close to a skirmish. While the dispute in 1967 had spiralled into a conflict at the border, in 2017, despite both countries possessing far greater military capabilities than before, the disagreement ended with a resolution through diplomatic channels. The reality of hostilities between nuclear-armed neighbours, who are also large economic powers, imposes costs of war which are far too monumental to absorb and sustain.[62] Conflict between the two ambitious neighbours is, however, likely to continue in various other strategic forms – via posturing, surrogate tussles in the neighbourhood and by vying for influence in the Indian Ocean and among smaller states.

The course of the Doklam dispute is fundamentally connected to the Nathu La and Cho La battles of 1967. At the heart of the Doklam dispute is China's desire for access to the Siliguri Corridor – the reason Sagat chose to continue to occupy Nathu La and not withdraw from the watershed. Gaining control over Doklam would give China access to the Jampheri ridge, which can be used to target the vulnerable Siliguri Corridor. Though the actual probability of a Chinese attack on the Siliguri Corridor from the Jampheri ridge is a vastly reduced one today, after the integration of Sikkim in 1975, such a situation would still pose a security dilemma for India.

The two separate incidents at Doklam – in 1966 and 2017 – are useful pointers to understand the stances of both countries over a period of time.[63] In 1966 and 1967, Chinese forces believed that they could 'teach India a lesson'. But after the battles of 1967 there has been a marked change in the approach to resolving disagreements, influenced by several factors. According to MacFarquhar's study of the country's history, China had realized by 1968, after the Cho La and Nathu La battles, that it would not be able to trounce India like in the war in 1962, but instead a conflict would result in incremental wins for both sides. The battles of 1967 gave India the confidence that it could challenge China successfully.

There have been other important reasons too for India and China not fighting a war again, which include the treaties of 1993, 1996 and the standard operating procedures (SOPs) of 2007 that have laid down drills for both sides, now nuclear powers, to prevent a recurrence of 1967. The 1993 agreement emphasizes that the two sides will jointly check and determine the segments on the border where they have points of difference.[64] An agreement signed in 1996 says that the two sides 'exchange maps indicating their respective perceptions of the entire alignment of the line of actual control as soon as possible'. SOPs were created in 2007, which require the soldiers to remain apart, and unfurl banners in two languages that tell the other patrol that it has crossed the border. The SOPs mandate that in the instance of a lack of clarity, both patrols will disengage and withdraw to their permanent locations. Over the years, though things on ground have turned difficult, diplomatic dialogue and detente have prevented edgy situations from boiling over (which include the several stand-offs at Doklam, Depsang and Chumar). Defence analyst Ajai Shukla believes that both sides are aware of their strengths and thus each side's patrols dominate the opposing side, wherever the terrain favours them along the vast LAC.[65]

The victory of 1967 is the precursor that restored parity between neighbours and set them on their journey towards ending wars. Fifty years and more have passed since the battles of 1967 and the two countries have never fought militarily again.

The closest that the two sides came to a fight was in Sumdorong Chu in 1986. It is instructive to understand how the parity restored twenty years earlier had transformed India's approach and China's response to it then too.

~

By 1986, two decades had passed in peace, when the calm was almost disrupted in the Sumdorong Chu region, north of Tawang in Arunachal Pradesh. This comes in the area of the Thagla Ridge[66] – the symbol of the 1962 disaster.

After capturing territories on the Indian side in the 1962 war, the PLA had withdrawn to its pre-war position north of the McMahon Line (the border). In June 1986, when an Indian intelligence detachment returned to occupy its forward post they found the post in the Sumdorong Chu area, south of the Thag La–Bum La ridge and considered by India to be part of its territory, to be occupied by forty Chinese soldiers who were erecting defence structures in the area.

Lieutenant General V.N. Sharma reported the development to General Krishnaswami Sundarji, the army chief, and recommended aggressive action to push back the Chinese. Bureaucrats in the foreign ministry in Delhi were advocating that if India withdraw a kilometre, so would the Chinese. The mutual withdrawals were meant to avoid an unnecessary eyeball to eyeball confrontation.

Initially, the chief too differed with Sharma, but the latter made an irrefutable, rational point. In case of a withdrawal, the Chinese could pull back a few kilometers to the Tibetan plateau yet swiftly return to occupy the forward position, whenever they wanted to, via well-established roads on the Tibet side, whereas the Indian army, once withdrawn, had to contend with crossing three ridges on foot to return to the position if needed, given the lack of roads and infrastructure on their own side. There was no chance that the Indian army could hope to displace any future Chinese occupation of that land, once any withdrawal of troops was made. The two contrasting cases of Jelep La (nervous withdrawal) and

Nathu La (stubborn occupation) in 1965 were staring at them as choices from history. Despite pressure from the government in Delhi, Sharma refused to withdraw, stating that under the constitution, he was bound by the duty to defend the territorial integrity of the country. He even offered to resign if he was asked to withdraw his troops.[67] Sundarji sided with his outspoken and bold Eastern Army commander over the bureaucrats in Delhi. It was a throwback to 1965 and the occupation of Nathu La, when Sagat had refused to withdraw and defied similar orders of his superiors.

Convinced by Sharma's compelling argument General Sundarji ordered Operation Falcon[68] to be set in motion – this was a strategic military plan involving a heavy forward deployment from Turtok in Ladakh to the India–Tibet–Burma trijunction. In a stunningly aggressive action, Sundarji brought an entire brigade to Zimithang (south of the India–China border) using Russian M26 helicopters and Indian forces took up positions on the Hathung La ridge, across the Namka Chu river. Sundarji then chose the vantage points to dominate: a helipad was constructed on a hilltop overlooking the Sumdorong Chu valley, heavy guns were brought in and emplaced and long-range patrols were soon roaming the area, surrounding the Chinese.

The Chinese responded by mobilizing forces and

soon, the two sides were close to a conflict again.[69] The difference was that while in 1962 the Chinese had held the first-mover advantage, in 1986 it was the Indians who had the upper hand by mobilizing their troops quicker.

General Sundarji had managed to put the Chinese on the defensive. Prime Minister Rajiv Gandhi's advisers complained that Sundarji's recklessness was responsible for the tensions. But the general stood firm, at one point telling a senior Rajiv aide, 'Please make alternate arrangements if you think you are not getting adequate professional advice.' Like Sagat had done earlier, the wily general refused to back off after acquiring an early edge even though the civilian government was discomfited.

Prime Minister Rajiv Gandhi, getting mixed signals from the bureaucracy and the military, decided to visit the forward areas including Tawang. At a forward post, after addressing the troops, he asked them if they would like to hold the forward area at Sumdorong Chu or vacate. To Rajiv's surprise, the troops boldly replied that instead they were getting ready to push the Chinese back and march into their territory, if ordered. The prime minister smiled and nodded to the troops. He had got his answer and was now confident of maintaining the aggressive posture.[70] The generals – Sundarji and Sharma – had been vindicated. It was an example of how decisions of local commanders could help a fair-minded prime minister with an ear to the ground overcome obfuscated thinking in faraway Delhi.

As Bertil Lintner writes in his book *China's India War*, 'It was extremely rare for an Indian army officer to challenge an elected government the way Sundarji did.' The civilians backed off, so did the Chinese. General V.N. Sharma, who became the next army chief, fondly remembers: 'We were on our territory and any withdrawal orders by government or army headquarters would be considered illegal as the army was tasked to defend India's border.'[71] In a rerun of 1967, India's army had got the better of China's PLA who were forced to withdraw.

The Sumdorong Chu incident unnerved the Chinese and precipitated an invite from the Chinese premier for Rajiv Gandhi, the Indian prime minister, to visit Peking. Rajiv Gandhi's visit to China in 1988 helped to defuse tensions.[72] The initial strategy of softening the enemy's stance through a limited military action had helped create the right atmosphere for a subsequent political rapprochement. Lintner further writes that after the Sumdorong Chu incident, the Chinese were far more careful in their dealings with India.[73] Twenty years after the battles at Nathu La and Cho La, the military used the aggressive defence posture of surprise and speed from Sagat Singh's playbook. Not vacating ground but continuing to proactively press the Chinese was a stubborn tactic used by Sagat from 1965 to 1967. Two decades later, Sundarji and Sharma used speed to wrest key vantage points on ground and pin Chinese forces. The underpinning tactic of wresting psychological advantage early was key to dominating China in both 1967 and 1986.

Like in 1967, and then again in 1986–87, the Indian army's power play and aggression rattled the PLA, which led to the sacking of its Tibet military district commander and military region chief in Chengdu.[74] India had taken a strong stand against a Chinese threat and called the bluff, just like it had done in Sikkim in 1967. Two decades after Sagat had disagreed with his superiors, Sundarji took on bureaucrats who had a poor understanding of the area and even worse understanding of the psychological nature of the stand-off. On both occasions, the generals had been proven right.

The harsh lesson that emerges from the battles of 1967 was that battlefield decisions are best left to generals with a better handle over military matters. Krishna Menon, the defence minister in 1962, often undermined the value of inputs from generals on war and meddled in military decision-making, which resulted in disastrous outcomes.

But it is also important to recognize the inflection point at which political overtures need to replace military responses since they decide the larger trajectory of strategic objectives of peace and conflict. After the battle of Nathu La was over, Sagat had planned to launch an attack on China, as mentioned earlier in the book. It is at this point that the government in Delhi took a sagacious political decision to prevent reckless military adventure.

A political decision must be supreme and any military decision must be subordinate to it. However, political moves are most impactful when made from a position of relative strength, which can only be acquired through an early initiative and often involve military means. The battles of 1967 and subsequent incidents such as Sumdorong Chu help us understand that there is no substitute to obtaining early but limited demonstrable robust military advantage with China to enable the attainment of higher strategic goals.

India's responses to aggressive stances until 1967 had been cautious, complicated and, often, timid. The battles of 1967 had, for the first time, witnessed India react without self-doubt and dilemma. M. Taylor Fravel, a military historian, further makes a point that there has been a declining claim strength and consequent negative shifts in China's bargaining power to escalate territorial disputes. He believes this factor was evident both in 1967 and in 1986.[75]

The battles of 1967 were also the turning point after which China has never weighed in with active military support for Pakistan, like it did in 1965. Since that time, it became apparent that China was unwilling to fight other nations' battles.

~

The battles of 1967 were indeed the harbinger of a lasting peace, a peace that is, according to military folklore, safeguarded by the spirit of a departed soldier.

A year after the Nathu La–Cho La battles, in 1968, a section of soldiers, escorting a mule column on patrol from Tuku La to Dongchui La[76] in Sikkim were hit by a severe storm. The patrol managed to return to the base, but not before it had lost Sepoy Harbhajan Singh, a young soldier from the 23rd Battalion of the Punjab Regiment. Harbhajan slipped and fell into a mountain stream and the current swept his body downstream. His body was found after a rigorous three-day search and cremated with full military honours.

A few days later Harbhajan appeared in the dream of one of the senior army officers, entreating him to build a memorial for him, which was soon constructed. The story of Harbhajan turned into a legend.

The memorial evolved into a shrine where soldiers and travellers from faraway places came to pay homage and pray for their safety. Harbhajan became a 'baba', protecting those who served in the mountains. The legend grew over the years. Devotees came to believe that Harbhajan slept on a camp bed provided for him by the army, and each morning, the sheets, magically crumpled overnight, were changed, his boots polished and his uniforms readied.

After his death, Baba Harbhajan was promoted up the military ranks, to a junior commissioned officer, and a salary cheque was sent to his family every month. He was even granted annual leave and a berth on the train to his native town of Kapurthala in Punjab would be reserved for his travel. On 14 September each year, a train would leave New Jalpaiguri station in West Bengal, carrying soldiers taking the belongings of Baba Harbhajan and bringing them back the same way. This was done every year until he 'retired' a few years ago.

The Indian and Chinese soldiers who gave up their lives in the battles of Nathu La and Cho La had fought to protect their respective countries. Most of them will be forgotten in time. Baba Harbhajan, who fell during a routine border patrol in the harsh terrain, will be remembered in death more than in life, and in the decades to follow, Baba would come to share a deep connect with the soldiers, both Indian and Chinese, in the Sikkim Himalayas.

Soldiers believe that the Nathu La pass is guarded by the ghost of Baba Harbhajan, protector of the 3,000-odd men of the Nathu La brigade watching over the 14,000-foot-high border point with China, who gives them a three-day advance notice of any attack![77]

He is in a sense a beacon of hope for peace between India and China. When the Chinese arrive at Nathu La to attend flag meetings with their Indian counterparts, they leave a seat vacant on their side for Baba Harbhajan as a sign of respect.

In these Himalayan heights where death can arrive at any moment and survival is a blessing, soldiers on both sides pray for peace. Baba Harbhajan is that hope for peace and friendship, loved and respected by soldiers on both sides of the border.

~

Close to five hundred men died in Nathu La and Cho La in the fall of 1967. About a thousand ended up injured on both sides. No one has fired a bullet in the Nathu La and Cho La regions ever since. India and China haven't fought a battle in over fifty years.[78]

Notes

Chapter 1: Secret Games: Spies, Soldiers and the Opening Gambit

1. Clarridge, Duane. *A Spy For All Seasons: My Life in the CIA.* Scribner, 2002.
2. Mazzetti, Mark, 'Former Spy with Agenda Operates the C.I.A.,' *New York Times*, 22 January 2011, https://www.nytimes.com/2011/01/23/world/23clarridge.html?hp=&pagewanted=all
3. Mazzetti, Mark, 'Brash Spy Who Fought Terror Networks Dies at 83,' *New York Times*, 10 April 2016, https://www.nytimes.com/2016/04/11/us/duane-r-clarridge-brash-spy-who-fought-terror-dies-at-83.html
4. Weil, Martin, 'Duane "Dewey" Clarridge, CIA official enmeshed in Iran-contra affair, dies at 83,' *Washington Post*, 11 April 2016, https://www.washingtonpost.com/national/duane-dewey-clarridge-cia-official-enmeshed-in-iran-contra-affair-dies-at-83/2016/04/11/78979470-ff90-11e5-9203-7b8670959b88_story.html?utm_term=.79e7835206d6

5. Ibid.

6. Ibid.

7. Ibid.

8. Manoj Joshi, https://www.orfonline.org/research/political-and-diplomatic-overview-of-the-run-up-to-the-1965-india-pakistan-war/

9. Praveen Swami. *India Pakistan and the Secret Jihad: The Covert war in Kashmir 1947–2004.*

10. Clarridge, Duane. *A Spy For All Seasons: My Life in the CIA.* Scribner, 2002.

11. Ibid.

12. Giffin, Sydney. *The Crisis Game: Simulating International Conflict.* New York: Doubleday and Company, 1965.

13. Ibid.

14. Ibid.

15. Bajwa, Farooq. *From Kutch to Tashkent: The Indo-Pakistan War of 1965.* Hurst, 2013. 38.

16. Abdullah had founded The Plebiscite Front which was banned. Abdullah's presence in Kashmir with the Plebiscite Front was considered a threat by the government. Finally, he merged the front into a revamped National Conference party in the 1970s.

17. Riedel, Bruce. *JFK's Forgotten Crisis: Tibet, the CIA, and the Sino-Indian War.* Harper Collins, 2015. 164.

18. Ganguly, Sumit. *Conflict Unending: India Pakistan Tensions since 1947.* New York: Columbia University Press, 2002. 37.

19. A squadron in air force is a unit comprising a number of aircrafts and their aircrews, usually of the same type.

20. Ganguly, Sumit. *Conflict Unending: India Pakistan Tensions*

since 1947. New York: Columbia University Press, 2002. 37.

21. Ibid.

22. https://timesofindia.indiatimes.com/india/The-rifle-that-won-the-war-in-1965/articleshow/49327325.cms

23. https://web.archive.org/web/20110609073650/http://www.bharat-rakshak.com/LAND-FORCES/Army/History/1965War/PDF/1965Chapter01.pdf

24. https://medium.com/@kbahmad05/27-december-1963-revisiting-the-sacrilege-c9141aaf6482

25. Bajwa, Farooq. *From Kutch to Tashkent: The Indo-Pakistan War of 1965.* Hurst, 2013. 34.

26. http://www.openthemagazine.com/article/voices/how-the-pandit-lost-the-valley

27. https://indianexpress.com/article/explained/karnataka-assembly-elections-narendra-modi-general-k-s-thimayya-vk-krishna-menon-5165987/

28. Dasgupta, Amit and Lorenzo Luthi (edited). *The Sino-Indian War of 1962, p127: 'A British Defence Coordination Committee assessed that Pakistan may have been preying on India's inability to reach or defend the claim line of Ladakh.*

29. https://indianexpress.com/article/explained/karnataka-assembly-elections-narendra-modi-general-k-s-thimayya-vk-krishna-menon-5165987/

30. Bajwa, Farooq. *From Kutch to Tashkent: The Indo-Pakistan War of 1965.* Hurst, 2013. 38.

31. Altaf Gauhar, then Pakistan Minister of Information and Broadcasting and author of the biography Ayub Khan: *Pakistan's First Military Ruler.*

32. There are different versions regarding the total number of

infiltrating groups. Pakistani scholar Farooq Bajwa, in his book From Kutch to Tashkent: The Indo-Pakistan War of 1965, mentions six groups. However, the story here mentions 7 groups, using Major General Afsir Karim's version. Afsir Karim fought in the 1965 war.

33. http://in.rediff.com/news/2005/sep/19war.htm

34. Ceasefire Line was later redesignated as the 'Line of Control (LoC)' following the Simla Agreement, which was signed between India and Pakistan on 3 July 1972. CFL was the unofficial boundary that divided the two countries, now represented by LoC or LC.

35. Garver, John W. *Protracted Contest: Sino-Indian Rivalry in the Twentieth Century*. University of Washington Press, 2011.

36. Brigadier (retd) Shaukat Qadir says, 'Far from rising up in arms, the local population denied any support and, in many instances, handed over the infiltrators to Indian troops.'

37. For instance, when the Salahuddin force (one of the infiltrating columns) was crossing the Pir Panjal ranges, they tried to bribe a Kashmiri Gujjar shepherd named Mohammed Din, in exchange for safe passage into the Kashmir valley. Instead, Mohammed Din, suspicious of their unusual movements, reported the matter to the state's criminal investigations department where its head Pir Ghulam Hassan Shah, swiftly passed the information to the state's home minister D.P. Dhar, leading to the Salahuddin force being identified and tackled by Indian military forces.

38. Pradhan, R.D. *The Inside Story: 1965 War, The Inside Story – Defence Minister YB Chavan's Diary of India-Pakistan War.* Atlantic Publishers & Dist, 2007.10.

39. Ibid.
40. Y.B. Chavan was told that India weapons were fit for the museum by the US senator.
41. https://economictimes.indiatimes.com/news/defence/1965-war-when-foot-soldiers-took-on-the-mighty-pattons-of-pakistan/articleshow/49032326.cms?from=mdr
42. Pradhan, R D. *The Inside Story: 1965 War, The Inside Story – Defence Minister YB Chavan's Diary of India-Pakistan War.* Atlantic Publishers & Dist, 2007. 33.
43. Riedel, Bruce. *JFK's Forgotten Crisis: Tibet, the CIA, and the Sino-Indian War.* Harper Collins, 2015, 166.
44. Bisht, Rachna. *1965: Stories from the Second Indo-Pakistan War.* Penguin India, 2015.
45. Unofficial estimates put the number beyond 10.
46. https://timesofindia.indiatimes.com/city/lucknow/Pak-tanks-stopped-shelling-as-mark-of-respect-to-my-father/articleshow/49189205.cms
47. Pradhan, R D. *The Inside Story: 1965 War, The Inside Story – Defence Minister YB Chavan's Diary of India-Pakistan War.* Atlantic Publishers & Dist, 2007. 65.
48. Pradhan, R D. *The Inside Story: 1965 War, The Inside Story – Defence Minister YB Chavan's Diary of India-Pakistan War.* Atlantic Publishers & Dist, 2007. 96.

Chapter 2: In the Shadow of the Dragon: The War Moves East

1. 'Nathula Pass,' *Sikkim STDC,* http://www.sikkimstdc.com/GeneralPages/Details/Nathula-%20Pass/215/Details.aspx

2. Duff, Andrew. *Sikkim: A Requiem for A Himalayan Kingdom.* London: Penguin Books, 2016, 31.

3. Datta-Ray, Sunanda K. *Smash and Grab: Annexation of Sikkim.* Vikas, 1984, 84.

4. Duff, Andrew. *Sikkim: A Requiem for A Himalayan Kingdom.* London: Penguin Books, 2016, 44.

5. Duff, Andrew. *Sikkim: A Requiem for A Himalayan Kingdom.* London: Penguin Books, 2016, 52.

6. In 2003 that there was a thaw in bilateral relations after then prime minister Atal Bihari Vajpayee visited China, which resulted in an agreement on opening up Nathu La for trade with China. The border trade officially started from 2006 and continued for six months (May–November 2013).

7. Namka Chu is a river that flows near the Tawang district in the Indian state of Arunachal Pradesh. Namka Chu valley was the place of initial fighting between India and China in 1962.

8. Sinh, Randhir. *A Talent for War: The Military Biography of Lt Gen Sagat Singh.* Vij Books India, 2013, 66.

9. Sinh, Randhir. *A Talent for War: The Military Biography of Lt Gen Sagat Singh.* Vij Books India, 2013, 44.

10. Codenamed Operation Vijay, the Indian army used a two-pronged attack, using army on land, the navy to blockade the ports of Margao, Vasco and Daman and the air force was tasked to destroy the two airfields at Dambolim and Bambolim and provide air support to troops. The Portuguese presence consisted of about 5,000 soldiers in Goa, and over a 1,000 across Daman and Diu, three infantry battalions and

one wheeled armoured car squadron, a naval frigate and two transport air force planes.

11. Sinh, Randhir. *A Talent for War: The Military Biography of Lt Gen Sagat Singh*. Vij Books India, 2013, 69.

12. Sinh, Randhir. *A Talent for War: The Military Biography of Lt Gen Sagat Singh*. Vij Books India, 2013, 70.

13. Pradhan, R D. *The Inside Story: 1965 War, The Inside Story – Defence Minister YB Chavan's Diary of India-Pakistan War*. Atlantic Publishers & Dist, 2007, 65.

14. Pradhan, R D. *The Inside Story: 1965 War, The Inside Story – Defence Minister YB Chavan's Diary of India-Pakistan War*. Atlantic Publishers & Dist, 2007, 66.

15. Riedel, Bruce. *JFK's Forgotten Crisis: Tibet, the CIA, and the Sino-Indian War*. Harper Collins, 2015, 166.

16. Office of the Historian, US Department of State, Foreign Relations of the United States, 1964–68, 'Prospects of Chinese Communist Involvement in the Indo-Pakistan War,' Vol XXV, South Asia, Document 205, Special National Intelligence Estimate, SNIE 13-1065, 16 September 1965.

17. After the 1962 war, India took assistance from the US and the UK to provide military supplies to the Indian Army. India also began to strengthen relations with the Soviet Union for assistance. US President Lyndon Johnson preferred to stay away from the war since he was also occupied with the Vietnam war.

18. Arpi, Claude, 'Notes, Documents and Letters Exchanged between the government of India and China: January 1965– February 1966,' White Paper XII, Government of India.

http://www.claudearpi.net/wp-content/uploads/2016/12/WhitePaper12NEW.pdf

19. Declassified CIA files.

20. Kalyanaraman, S, 'The Context of the Cease-Fire Decision in the 1965 India-Pakistan War,' *Institute for Defence Studies and Analyses*, 21 September 2015, https://idsa.in/specialfeature/TheContextoftheCeaseFireDecisioninthe1965_skalyanaraman_210915

21. Bajpai, G.C. *China's Shadow over Sikkim: The Politics of Intimidation*. Spantech & Lancer, 1999, 154.

Chapter 3: Protests, Disagreements and a Temporary Truce: Advantage China

1. Katoch, Ghyanshyam, 'The 1965 Chinese Ultimatum – A Bird's Eye View of Coercion,' *Centre for Land Warfare Studies*, 7 September 2015, https://archive.claws.in/1432/the-1965-chinese-ultimatum-a-birds-eye-view-of-coercion-ghanshyam-katoch.html

2. Arpi, Claude, 'A World War over some sheeps and a few Yaks?,' *Indian Defence Review*, 3 July 2017, http://www.indiandefencereview.com/a-world-war-over-some-sheeps-and-a-few-yaks

3. Arpi, Claude, 'Notes, Documents and Letters Exchanged between the government of India and China: January 1965–February 1966,' White Paper XII, Government of India. http://www.claudearpi.net/wp-content/uploads/2016/12/WhitePaper12NEW.pdf

4. Ibid.

5. 'When Atal Bihari Vajpayee exposed China's designs with

a flock of sheep,' *Economic Times*, 5 July 2017, https://
economictimes.indiatimes.com/news/politics-and-nation/
when-atal-behari-vajpayee-exposed-chinas-designs-with-
a-flock-of-sheep/articleshow/59453326.cms

6. The note was a strongly worded one. It said: In the afternoon
of September 24, 1965, a mob of Indian hooligans went to
the gate of the Chinese Embassy in New Delhi to make
provocation led by Indian officials and Congress leaders
and driving a flock of sheep before them. They made a huge
din, yelling that China had 'invented absurd pretexts for
threatening and intimidating India' that 'China wants to start
a world war over some sheep and a few yaks', and so on and
so forth.

7. Arpi, Claude, 'Notes, Documents and Letters Exchanged
between the government of India and China: January 1965–
February 1966,' White Paper XII, Government of India.
http://www.claudearpi.net/wp-content/uploads/2016/12/
WhitePaper12NEW.pdf

8. Arpi, Claude, 'A World War over some sheeps and a few
Yaks?,' *Indian Defence Review*, 3 July 2017, http://www.
indiandefencereview.com/a-world-war-over-some-sheeps-
and-a-few-yaks

9. The Indian note further added: In March 1959, when
the Dalai Lama fled from Lhasa, following the Chinese
invasion of Tibet, and took asylum in India, the Chinese
Government had stated that His Holiness was 'abducted to
India by Tibetan rebels' and kept under duress by the Indian
authorities.

10. Chawla, Prabhu, 'Historic visit to China by Prime

Minister Vajpayee brings Beijing and Delhi closer,' *India Today*, 7 July 2003, https://www.indiatoday.in/magazine/neighbours/story/20030707-historic-visit-to-china-by-prime-minister-vajpayee-brings-beijing-and-delhi-closer-792525-2003-07-07

11. Note written by Lieutenant Colonel Lakhpat Singh, staff officer to Lieutenant General Sagat Singh at 17 Division.

12. Notes of Brigadier (retd) Lakhpat Singh.

13. The Line of Actual Control (LAC) is the effective border between India and China spanning almost 4057 kilometres.

14. 11 Jak Rifles battalion was part of 112 Mountain Brigade, 17 Mountain Division. The other battalions of the brigade were 17 Maratha Light Infantry (at Nathu La 14,000 feet) and 5 Bihar in depth.

15. Katoch, Ghyanshyam, 'The 1965 Chinese Ultimatum – A Bird's Eye View of Coercion,' *Centre for Land Warfare Studies*, 7 September, 2015, https://archive.claws.in/1432/the-1965-chinese-ultimatum-a-birds-eye-view-of-coercion-ghanshyam-katoch.html

16. Katoch, Ghyanshyam, 'The 1965 Chinese Ultimatum – A Bird's Eye View of Coercion,' *Centre for Land Warfare Studies*, 7 September 2015, https://archive.claws.in/1432/the-1965-chinese-ultimatum-a-birds-eye-view-of-coercion-ghanshyam-katoch.html

17. http://www.claws.in/images/journals_doc/2042471866_VKSingh.pdf

18. The McMahon Line is the demarcation line between the Tibetan region of China and the north-east region of India proposed by British colonial administrator Henry

McMahon at the 1914 Simla Convention. It is regarded as the international boundary between China and India, although its legal status is disputed by the Chinese government.

19. Sinh, Randhir. *A Talent for War: The Military Biography of Lt Gen Sagat Singh.* Vij Books India, 2013, 74.

20. Garver, John W. *Protracted Contest: Sino-Indian Rivalry in the Twentieth Century.* University of Washington Press, 2011, 96.

21. Garver, John W. *Protracted Contest: Sino-Indian Rivalry in the Twentieth Century.* University of Washington Press, 2011, 96.

22. Sinh, Randhir. *A Talent for War: The Military Biography of Lt Gen Sagat Singh.* Vij Books India, 2013, 75.

23. http://www.claws.in/images/journals_doc/2042471866_VKSingh.pdf

24. Sinh, Randhir. *A Talent for War: The Military Biography of Lt Gen Sagat Singh.* Vij Books India, 2013.

25. Wallis Simpson had married Britain's King Edward VII, which led him to relinquish the crown in December 1936. Rita Hayworth, the former actress married Prince Aly Khan – the son of Aga Khan III, then spiritual lead of Ismaili Muslims after her break-up to actor director Orson Welles (courtesy: Andrew Duff on Sikkim).

26. Duff, Andrew. *Sikkim: A Requiem for A Himalayan Kingdom.* London: Penguin Books, 2016.

27. Cooke, Hope. *Time Change: An Autobiography.* Berkley, 1982.

28. Cooke, Hope. *Time Change: An Autobiography.* Berkley, 1982, 145.

29. Conversations with Lieutenant Colonel K.B. Joshi.

30. Duff, Andrew. *Sikkim: A Requiem for A Himalayan Kingdom.* London: Penguin Books, 2016.

31. Cooke, Hope. *Time Change: An Autobiography*. Berkley, 1982. 144.

32. Datta-Ray, Sunanda K. *Smash and Grab: Annexation of Sikkim*. Vikas, 1984, 50.

33. Bajwa, Farooq. *From Kutch to Tashkent: The Indo-Pakistan War of 1965*. Hurst Publishers, 2013, 352.

34. McLeod, Duncan. *India and Pakistan: Friends, Rivals or Enemies?* Routledge, 2008, 88.

35. Ibid.

36. Bajwa, Farooq. *From Kutch to Tashkent: The Indo-Pakistan War of 1965*. Hurst Publishers, 2013.

37. In the following years, the US, under President Richard Nixon and his foreign secretary, Henry Kissinger, returned to the Pakistani camp, driven by Cold War sentiments.

38. Garver, John W. *Protracted Contest: Sino-Indian Rivalry in the Twentieth Century*. University of Washington Press, 2011, 203.

Chapter 4: China's Psychological Tactics: Softening Up the Enemy Before the Storm

1. Lintner, Bertil. *Great Game East: India, China and the Struggle for Asia's Most Volatile Frontier*. Harper Collins, 2012, 112.

2. Deb, Sandipan, 'Naxalbari: Home to the Revolution,' *Outlook India*, 8 January, 2001, https://www.outlookindia.com/magazine/story/naxalbari-home-to-the-revolution/210639.

3. Lintner, Bertil. *China's India War: Collision Course on the Roof of the World*. Oxford University Press, 2018, 140-141.

4. Ibid.

5. 'Spring Thunder Over India,' *Marxists*, 5 July 1967, https://www.marxists.org/subject/china/documents/peoples-daily/1967/07/05.htm

6. 'Don't copy us, Mao had told Indian Maoists' *Business Standards*, 22 August 2014, https://www.business-standard.com/article/news-ians/don-t-copy-us-mao-had-told-indian-maoists-114082200217_1.html

7. Lintner, Bertil. *China's India War: Collision Course on the Roof of the World*. Oxford University Press, 2018, 137.

8. There were disagreements within the communist party of India and the radicals accused the party leadership of embracing revisionism. When communist party purged the radicals, the latter group went on to form the CPI(ML). The CPI(ML) advocated armed revolution and denounced participation in the electoral process.

9. MacFarquhar, Roderick and John K. Fairbank, ed. *The Cambridge History of China, The People's Republic, Part 2: Revolutions within the Chinese Revolution, 1966-1982*. Cambridge University Press, 1991, 251.

10. Cooke, Hope. *Time Change: An Autobiography*. Berkley, 1982. 198.

11. Marshall, Julie G. and Alastair Lamb. *Britain and Tibet 1765-1947: A Select Annotated Bibliography of British Relations with Tibet and the Himalayan States Including Nepal, Sikkim and Bhutan*. Psychology Press, 2005, 195.

12. Ghose, Sagarika. *Indira: India's Most Powerful Prime Minister*. Juggernaut Books, 2017.

13. Ibid.

14. Sinh, Randhir. *A Talent for War: The Military Biography of Lt Gen Sagat Singh.* Vij Books India, 2013.

15. Article 1 of the border treaty of 1890 states that 'the boundary of Sikkim and Tibet shall be the crest of the mountain range separating the waters flowing into the Sikkim Teesta and its affluents from the waters flowing into the Tibetan Mochu and northwards into other rivers of Tibet. The line commences at Mount Gipmochi, on the Bhutan frontier, and follows the above-mentioned water-parting to the point where it meets Nepal territory.'

16. Patranobis, Sutirtho, 'Genesis of a border stand-off: When China attacked Indira Gandhi in 1966 for supporting Bhutan,' *Hindustan Times*, 3 July 2017, https://www.hindustantimes. com/india-news/genesis-of-a-border-standoff-when-china-attacked-indira-gandhi-in-1966-for-supporting-bhutan/ story-BzCLTnwkV2ioO2ueJkUi6N.html

17. CIA report, 1967.

18. Ibid.

19. 'China: Nuclear,' *NTI*, April, 2015, https://www.nti.org/learn/ countries/china/nuclear

Chapter 5: 1966-67: Warriors Arrive at the Watershed

1. Of the ten Gurkha regiments in the British army, the 2nd, 6th, 7th and 10th regiments were transferred to Britain. The rest – 1st, 3rd, 4th, 5th, 8th and 9th – were inducted into the Indian army.

2. From the 7th and 10th Gurkha regiments allotted to the British army, a large number of soldiers expressed their desire to stay back in India. These boys came from the Rai

and Limbu tribes of the eastern hills in Nepal. The Gurkha regiments in India spelt the name as Gorkha (with an 'o' instead of a 'u').

3. Battalions in Gorkha Rifles are referred to with the battalion's named followed by the regiment. For instance 7/11 GR would mean the 7th battalion of 11 Gorkha Rifles regiment.

4. The Grenadiers regiment has an interesting origin story. The Grenadiers drew their name from the medieval wars, when the invention of rifles and cannons caused much concern. As a solution: grenadas (pomegranates) or grenade balls were filled with grapeshot and mixed with gunpowder on pieces of cord dipped in resin. A box of sulphur matchsticks or flints were packed in pouches attached to the cross belts of the men carrying them. The young men would step up to hurl these grenades from a distance at the enemy, causing large-scale casualties. The Grenadier (also called storm trooper) was a fighter who needed neither a rifle nor a gun. The enemy was often surprised by the sheer audacity of these close-range attacks, and soon other armies were employing the tactic successfully. By 1671, the French army had one grenadier company in every battalion and thereafter, Louis XV's household troops began to use horses too, which later became the Horse Grenadier Guards. The grenadiers marched on 'the right of the line' in an infantry battalion – which was a pride of place accorded to men who were waging a battle with bare hands.

5. The operational command of eastern region of India was under the Eastern Command of the armed forces, headquartered in Kolkata. 33 Corps, which was headquartered in Siliguri (West

Bengal), oversaw three divisions – 17 and 27 Division were in Sikkim while 20 Division was stationed in West Bengal.

6. Colonel Vishnu Sharma preceded K.B. Joshi as the commanding officer.

7. Conversation with K.B. Joshi.

8. 'Know your army: leadership,' *Indian Army*, https:// indianarmy.nic.in/Site/FormTemplete/frmTempSimple.as px?MnId=XldL/2bPGu1xeH6GTbfCNw==&ParentID=4l K1mX5lbt2F4vsBbeyMhw

9. Conversation with Narayan Parulekar.

10. An adjutant virtually functions as the chief operating officer (COO) of the battalion.

11. In field areas younger officers are often given higher responsibilities, given the paucity of officers.

12. There were several young untested but enthusiastic officers from all over India who lent the battalion an inclusive profile. Alongside Paru and Ram Singh, there was Samuel from Kerala, Pandey from Lucknow, Chopra, the hustling Punjabi from Delhi, and Bala Ganapathy, the quiet, stocky ex-army officer's son from Bangalore.

13. RCL guns are large guns that can be operated by one or two men. The recoil during firing the gun was softened or eclipsed by allowing part of the propelling blast to escape to the rear.

14. Conversations with Tinjong Lama in Lamahatta, Darjeeling.

15. Bellamy, Chris. *The Gurkhas: Special Force*. London: Hachette, 2011, 218.

16. Many years later, in the 2000s, while serving in a UN contingent in Africa, 2nd Grenadiers noticed a young officer named Raza posted in the same brigade in the UN, fighting

on the same side as them and against the rebels. Raza, who was Akram's son, was invited by the Grenadiers battalion to the officer's mess, where his father was felicitated and paid homage for being one of the bravest opponents. The young Raza, an upright officer, accepted the award from 2nd Grenadiers for his father in the traditions of soldiering.

17. Only the most competent officers were chosen to attend the prestigious Defence Services Staff College course at Camberley, England.

18. Conversations with Major General Randhir Sinh.

19. Palaka, Rambabu, 'Study of watershed characteristics using Google Elevation Service,' *Geospatial World*, 3 September 2016, https://www.geospatialworld.net/article/study-of-watershed-characteristics-using-google-elevation-service

20. http://www.claws.in/images/journals_doc/2042471866_VKSingh.pdf

Chapter 6: The Tipping Point: A Tale of Spies and a Breach at the Watershed

1. Menon, Vandana, and Chatterjee, Nayanika, 'Remembering the war we forgot: 51 years ago, how India gave China a bloody nose,' *Print*, 1 October 2018, https://theprint.in/defence/remembering-the-war-we-forgot-51-years-ago-how-india-gave-china-a-bloody-nose/127356

2. Menon, Vandana, and Chatterjee, Nayanika, 'Remembering the war we forgot: 51 years ago, how India gave China a bloody nose,' *Print*, 1 October 2018, https://theprint.in/defence/remembering-the-war-we-forgot-51-years-ago-how-india-gave-china-a-bloody-nose/127356

3. Ibid.

4. Jerome Alan Cohen, Hungdah Chiu, People's China and International Law, Volume 2: A Documentary Study, p1013

5. 'Indian diplomats humiliated at Peking airport,' *The Hindu*, 15 June, 2017, https://www.thehindu.com/archive/indian-diplomats-humiliated-at-peking-airport/article19050018.ece

6. Ibid.

7. Note 610. Given by the Embassy of India in China to the Ministry of Foreign Affairs, Peking, 9 November 1967.

8. Jerome Alan Cohen, Hungdah Chiu, People's China and International Law, Volume 2: A Documentary Study, p1008

9. Keesing's Record of World Events (Keesing's Worldwide LLC), Volume 13 September, 1967.

10. Ibid.

11. Conversations with Lieutenant Colonel K.B. Joshi and Major General Randhir Sinh.

12. According to Major General V.K. Singh, who served in the Sikkim sector at that time but was not involved in the battles.

13. http://www.claws.in/images/journals_doc/2042471866_VKSingh.pdf

14. https://indianarmy.nic.in/Site/FormTemplete/frmTempSimple.aspx?

15. http://www.claws.in/images/journals_doc/2042471866_VKSingh.pdf

Chapter 7: Hellfire at Nathu La

1. Mortars are lighter, simpler man portable weapons that can clear crests and obstacles due to the parabolic trajectory of

their rounds. Artillery guns have similar capability. However, in comparison to mortars, artillery guns constitute heavier equipment that are transported on vehicles and have longer range of delivery of their shells. Mortars are usually possessed by infantry battalions and are easier to operate. In comparison, artillery guns are more technically complex and need specialized regiments to handle, operate and manoeuvre.

2. Major Shaitan Singh Bhati, PVC was a recipient of Param Vir Chakra, India's highest gallantry decoration. In the battle of Rezang La in 1962, Shaitan Singh and 120 soldiers of a Kumaon battalion had successfully killed 1300 Chinese men and stopped the enemy advance. The incredible tale in a tragic war had spurred young boys such as Sheru at that time.

3. Conversations with Major General Sheru Thapliyal in Delhi.

4. Singh, General V.K., 'Nathu La 1967 – The Real Story,' *Veekay's History Book*, 4 April 2013, https://veekay-militaryhistory. blogspot.com/2013/04/nathula-1967-real-story.html.

5. Conversations with Bishan Singh in Jaipur.

6. Bishan Singh would later be transported to the Siliguri hospital as one of the survivors of Nathu La.

7. Conversations with Sheru Thapliyal in Delhi.

8. Sinh, Randhir. *A Talent for War: The Military Biography of Lt Gen Sagat Singh*. Vij Books India, 2013, 81.

9. https://theprint.in/defence/remembering-the-war-we-forgot-51-years-ago-how-india-gave-china-a-bloody-nose/127356/

10. Conversation with Major General Sheru Thapliyal.

11. http://veekay-militaryhistory.blogspot.com/2013/04/nathula-1967-real-story.html

12. Heavy casualties had been suffered by the 2nd Grenadiers in the battle, which was replaced by the 18th battalion of Rajput Regiment, of whom a platoon had fought at Nathu La.

13. Sinh, Randhir. *A Talent for War: The Military Biography of Lt Gen Sagat Singh*. Vij Books India, 2013, 81.

14. Madan, Tanvi, 'How the U.S. viewed the 1967 Sikkim skirmishes between India and China,' *Brookings*, 13 September, 2017, https://www.brookings.edu/opinions/ how-the-u-s-viewed-the-1967-sikkim-skirmishes-between- india-and-china

Chapter 8: The Battle of Cho La

1. Sharma, Gautam. *The Path of Glory: Exploits of the 11 Gorkha Rifles*. Allied Publishers, 1998, 66.

2. Ibid.

3. The four rifle companies of a battalion are known as A (alpha), B (bravo), C (charlie) and D (delta) companies.

4. Sharma, Gautam. *The Path of Glory: Exploits of the 11 Gorkha Rifles*. Allied Publishers, 1998, 66.

5. Sharma, Gautam. *The Path of Glory: Exploits of the 11 Gorkha Rifles*. Allied Publishers, 1998, 68.

6. Conversation with Lieutenant Colonel K.B. Joshi in Dehradun, April 2018.

7. Sharma, Gautam. *The Path of Glory: Exploits of the 11 Gorkha Rifles*. Allied Publishers, 1998, 66.

8. Sharma, Gautam. *The Path of Glory: Exploits of the 11 Gorkha Rifles*. Allied Publishers, 1998, 69.

9. Conversation with Lieutenant Colonel K.B. Joshi in Dehradun, April 2018.

10. Artillery comprises a class of weapons that are built to engage targets far beyond the range and power of infantry's small arms, which includes HMG, MMG and LMGs. Also, artillery guns can clear crest because of the parabolic trajectory of their fire. In contrast, the machine gun family has a lesser range and engages weapons in a direct trajectory – or a straight line – and is not designed to have a parabolic flight of its fire.

11. Sharma, Gautam. *The Path of Glory: Exploits of the 11 Gorkha Rifles*. Allied Publishers, 1998, 71.

12. Conversation with Lieutenant Colonel K.B. Joshi in Dehradun, April 2018.

13. Sharma, Gautam. *The Path of Glory: Exploits of the 11 Gorkha Rifles*. Allied Publishers, 1998, 71.

14. Ibid.

15. Magnesium flares emit a bright light into the sky, and burn for a longer duration than other flares, thus enabling armies to detect, expose and shoot down enemy movements in the dark.

16. Conversation with Captain Narayan Parulekar in Pune, 2018.

17. Conversation with Lieutenant Colonel K.B. Joshi in Dehradun, April 2018.

18. Ibid.

19. Ibid.

20. Disequilibrium: Thunderbolt and Lightning: https://m.dailyhunt.in/news/india/english/financial+chronicle-epaper-finance/disequilibrium+thunderbolt+and+lightning-newsid-94375292

21. Sharma, Gautam. *The Path of Glory: Exploits of the 11 Gorkha Rifles*. Allied Publishers, 1998, 72.

22. Gallantry honours sometimes do not reflect the full extent of a warrior's sacrifice. General V.N. Sharma told the author how the phrase of a gallantry act – 'going beyond the call of duty' is paradoxically breaking the rules of duty and exercising bravery of the highest order. Debi Prasad's action was unprecedented.

Epilogue: After the Watershed Battles

1. MacFarquhar, Roderick and John K. Fairbank, ed. *The Cambridge History of China, Vol. 15: The People's Republic, Part 2: Revolutions within the Chinese Revolution, 1966-1982.* Cambridge University Press, 1991, 251.

2. Zakir Hussain was the briefest serving president of India and also the first Muslim to hold the post.

3. Iyer, G.S., 'Mao's Smile Revisited: Some Observations,' *Chennai Centre for China Studies*, 2 December, 2009, https://www.c3sindia.org/archives/maos-smile-revisited-some-observations

4. Ibid.

5. Ibid.

6. Raghavan, Srinath. *1971 – A Global History of the Creation of Bangladesh.* Harvard University Press, 2013, 193.

7. http://shodhganga.inflibnet.ac.in/bitstream/10603/202829/10/10_chapter%205.pdf

8. MacFarquhar, Roderick and John K. Fairbank, ed. *The Cambridge History of China, Vol. 15: The People's Republic, Part 2: Revolutions within the Chinese Revolution, 1966-1982.* Cambridge University Press, 1991.

9. Raghavan, Srinath. *1971 – A Global History of the Creation of Bangladesh.* Harvard University Press, 2013, 191.

10. MacFarquhar, Roderick and John K. Fairbank, ed. *The Cambridge History of China, Vol. 15: The People's Republic, Part 2: Revolutions within the Chinese Revolution, 1966-1982.* Cambridge University Press, 1991.

11. Tsiu, Tsien-hua. *The Sino-Soviet border dispute in the 1970's.* Mosaic Press, 1983.

12. Ibid. The Soviet Union had increased its forces from 15 divisions to 21, including 8 tank divisions. Soviet regular combat forces increased to 30 divisions. In addition to long and inter mediate range nuclear forces the Soviets now deployed tactical nuclear missiles along the Sino Soviet border.

13. Tsiu, Tsien-hua. *The Sino-Soviet border dispute in the 1970's.* Mosaic Press, 1983, 44.

14. Gates, Robert M. *From the Shadows: The Ultimate Insider's Story of Five Presidents and How They Won the Cold War.* Simon and Schuster, 1996.

15. Peng Duhai had emerged as a strong contender to Mao. Soon, his son was found to be involved in anti-party activities and Peng's position in the party was no more assured. Besides, Mao never liked younger leaders challenging him for a position and Peng became a marked man. Realizing that he would never ever return to the power centre, Peng decided to leave China for good. He finally did fly out of China, never to return again. His plane had disappeared over Mongolia. Mao's intelligence chief Kang Sheng had aided in large scale purges that eliminated his opponents and enabled Mao to grow stronger domestically, but which included purging hundreds of PLA generals and officers that weakened China's

fighting capabilities. Internationally, Mao and China were boxed into an isolated corner.

16. Burns, John F., 'In Death, Zhou Enlai Is Still Beloved (But a Puzzle),' *New York Times*, 10 January 1986, https://www. nytimes.com/1986/01/10/world/in-death-zhou-enlai-is-still-beloved-but-a-puzzle.html

17. Riedel, Bruce. *JFK's Forgotten Crisis: Tibet, the CIA, and the Sino-Indian War*. Harper Collins, 2015, 95.

18. A fiery, charismatic leader and articulate speaker who drew large crowds wherever he went, Mujib's popularity had pushed the Punjabi-Pathan power cohorts in the west into a corner. Mujib was arrested and his party Awami League's activities were suspended ushering in a period of crisis in East Pakistan.

19. The army patrolled the streets of Dhaka, dragging out protestors and opposition leaders and gunning them down, grabbing dissenters and pro freedom activists from their homes and shooting them before their families, killing senior professors in Dhaka university. An ethnic cleansing of unimaginable proportions took place. Archer Blood, the American consul general in Dhaka, sent frantic cables to Washington DC, updating the US government with terrible news about the devastating developments. Blood and his wife witnessed the losses of several lives, including some who they had known personally, and the mayhem shocked the couple. His cables, however, were ignored.

20. Bass, Gary J. *Blood Telegram: India's Secret War in East Pakistan*. India: Penguin Random House, 2014.

21. Ibid.

22. Mukherjee, Anit. *The Absent Dialogue: Politicians, Bureaucrats, and the Military in India*. Oxford University Press, 2019.

23. In 1967, Sam was the Eastern army commander under whom Sagat had engineered a victory against Chinese.

24. Singh, Harbaksh. *In the Line of Duty: A Soldier Remembers*. Lancer Publishers, 2000.

25. Arpi, Claude, '1971 War: How the US tried to corner India,' *Rediff*, 26 December 2006, https://www.rediff.com/news/2006/dec/26claude.htm

26. Bass, Gary J. *Blood Telegram: India's Secret War in East Pakistan*. India: Penguin Random House, 2014, 238.

27. Garver, John W. *Protracted Contest: Sino-Indian Rivalry in the Twentieth Century*. University of Washington Press, 2011, 96.

28. Bass, Gary J. *Blood Telegram: India's Secret War in East Pakistan*. India: Penguin Random House, 2014, 301.

29. Henry Kissinger arrived at the Brooklyn house accompanied by his assistants George H.W. Bush and Alexander Haig.

30. Bass, Gary J. *Blood Telegram: India's Secret War in East Pakistan*. India: Penguin Random House, 2014, 302.

31. Bass, Gary J. *Blood Telegram: India's Secret War in East Pakistan*. India: Penguin Random House, 2014, 309.

32. Riedel, Bruce. *JFK's Forgotten Crisis: Tibet, the CIA, and the Sino-Indian War*. Harper Collins, 2015, 170.

33. Bass, Gary J. *Blood Telegram: India's Secret War in East Pakistan*. India: Penguin Random House, 2014, 310.

34. Bass, Gary J. *Blood Telegram: India's Secret War in East Pakistan*. India: Penguin Random House, 2014.

35. Subramaniam, Arjun. *India's Wars: A Military History, 1947-1971*. Harper Collins, 2016, 382.

36. Subramaniam, Arjun. *India's Wars: A Military History, 1947–1971*. Harper Collins, 2016, 435.

37. Duff, Andrew. *Sikkim: A Requiem for A Himalayan Kingdom*. London: Penguin Books, 2016, 4–5.

38. Sinh, Randhir. *A Talent for War: The Military Biography of Lt Gen Sagat Singh*. Vij Books India, 2013.

39. Conversations with Major General Randhir Sinh.

40. Ibid.

41. She was unlikely to have been a CIA spy, given that American intelligence had established local friends in the form of the sisters of the Chogyal – Coocoola and Coola – much before Hope arrived in Sikkim and was unlikely to have cultivated the support of a white queen in a controversial Indian state who was independent, tactless and even indiscreet, as her writing and actions had revealed.

42. Cooke, Hope. *Time Change: An Autobiography*. Berkley, 1982, 200.

43. Duff, Andrew. *Sikkim: A Requiem for A Himalayan Kingdom*. London: Penguin Books, 2016, 167.

44. RAW set up information cells inside Bangladesh that provided intelligence which enabled the local Mukti Bahini to protect its field operators and achieve goals of disrupting the government's organs such as transport, railways, offices.

45. Datta-Ray, Sunanda K. *Smash and Grab: Annexation of Sikkim*. Vikas, 1984, 236.

46. 'Book review: How demands for treaty revision kept surfacing?,' *Daily Hunt*, 10 November 2018, https://m. dailyhunt.in/news/india/english/financial+chronicle-epaper-

finance/book+review+how+demands+for+treaty+revision+ke
pt+surfacing-newsid-101146629

47. Cooke, Hope. *Time Change: An Autobiography*. Berkley, 1982.

48. Duff, Andrew. *Sikkim: A Requiem for A Himalayan Kingdom*. London: Penguin Books, 2016.

49. It was a reference to a local rebellion in the Naxalbari neighbourhood of Bengal. In the next few years, the communist revolution turned violent, travelled inland, sweeping across the state like a contagion and gathering hordes of students, teachers, youth activists and others in its support. The movement had taken the lives of government officials, families and other innocents, sending the state of West Bengal spiraling into unprecedented crisis. It was not difficult to imagine that the looming threat of Communist China that had been knocking on the doors of Sikkim from the outside had managed to indoctrinate many in India. Given the avowed deference and hero worship of Mao Zedong by their leaders Kanu Sanya and Charu Majumdar, the Naxalite movement had made no secret of its inspiration and connections.

50. Norbu, 'The American Who Would be Queen: The Story of Hope Cooke, Last Gyalmo (Queen) of Sikkim,' *Steemit*, https://steemit.com/life/@norbu/the-american-who-would-be-queen-the-story-of-hope-cooke-last-gyalmo-queen-of-sikkim

51. Shukla, Satyendra R. *Sikkim: The Story of Integration*. S. Chand, 1976, 206.

52. Hoon, Lieutenant General Prem Nath, 'Sikkim brigade,' *Hoon's Legacy*, http://www.hoonslegacy.com/sikkim-brigade

53. Ibid.
54. Mehta, Ashok K., 'The truth about Sikkim,' *Rediff,* 7 November 2002, https://www.rediff.com/news/2002/nov/07ashok.htm
55. 'If we bring a small country like Sikkim within our fold by using force, it would be like killing a fly with a bullet,' Jawaharlal Nehru in the *Statesman*, 3 June 1960.
56. Duff, Andrew. *Sikkim: A Requiem for A Himalayan Kingdom.* London: Penguin Books, 2016.
57. Doklam plateau is located in the Doklam area (as referred to in the statements of the Ministry of External Affairs and the Embassy of Bhutan in New Delhi). The Doklam plateau lies around 30 km to the north east of Dolam plateau
58. Chengappa, Raj, 'India-China standoff: All you need to know about Doklam dispute,' *India Today*, 7 July 2017, https://www.indiatoday.in/magazine/cover-story/story/20170717-india-china-bhutan-border-dispute-doklam-beijing-siliguri-corridor-1022690-2017-07-07
59. A lesser known outcome of that incident was the strengthening of ties between India and Bhutan.
60. Chanakya, 'Sikkim standoff: China is angry because India has changed the rules,' *Hindustan Times*, 16 July 2017, https://www.hindustantimes.com/analysis/sikkim-standoff-%20china-is-angry-because-india-has-changed-the-rules-of-%20the-game/story-KTfW5296YkNuDkguL1A3SN.html
61. https://www.thehindu.com/news/national/army-acted-fast-in-doklam-lt-gen-praveen-bakshi/article21383282.ece
62. Conflict between such neighbours is however likely to continue via posturing, surrogate tussles in the neighbourhood and in the Indian ocean.

63. The construction of the road clearly changes the security dynamics to our detriment significantly,' says Ashok Kantha, former envoy to China and director of the Institute of Chinese Studies in Delhi. 'They are changing the status quo in a very major way and it has serious security implications for us. The Chinese are changing the trijunction unilaterally, and this affects us as the Chinese military presence here will be widened and deepened.

64. The 1993 Agreement on the Maintenance of Peace Along the Line of Actual Control on the India–China Border mentions, 'When necessary, the two sides shall jointly check and determine the segments of the line of actual control where they have different views as to its alignment.'

65. Shukla, Ajai, 'Ajai Shukla: Seeing is perceiving,' *Business Standard*, 11 October 2013, https://www.business-standard.com/article/opinion/ajai- shukla-seeing-is-perceiving-113093001058_1.html

66. Situated east of Bhutan and north of the McMahon Line, Thagla Ridge is remembered for the start of the 1962 conflict.

67. Conversation with General V.N. Sharma.

68. Six years earlier, in 1980, General K.V. Krishna Rao had presented Indira Gandhi with a strategic military plan that envisaged a heavy forward deployment on the arc from Turtok (Ladakh) to the India–Tibet–Myanmar trijunction. Named Operation Falcon, the deployment was envisaged alongside building support infrastructure through a period of fifteen years.

69. Arpi, Claude, 'The Sumdorong Chu Incident: a strong Indian stand,' *Indian Defence Review*, 4 May 2013, http://www.

indiandefencereview.com/the-sumdorong-chu-incident-a-
strong-indian-stand

70. Conversation with General V.N. Sharma.

71. Chengappa, Bidanda M. *India-China relations: post conflict
phase to post Cold War Period.* The University of Michigan
Press: 2008, 83.

72. Cohen, Stephen P. and Sunil Dasgupta. *Arming without
Aiming: India's Military Modernization.* Brookings Institution,
2012, 13.

73. Lintner, Bertil. *China's India War: Collision Course on the Roof
of the World.* Oxford University Press, 2018, 265.

74. Joshi, Manoj, 'Operation Falcon: When General Sundarji
took the Chinese by surprise,' *ORF Online,* 3 July, 2017,
https://www.orfonline.org/research/operation-falcon-when-
general-sundarji-took-the-chinese-by-surprise.

75. Fravel, Taylor M. *Strong Borders, Secure Nation: Cooperation
and Conflict in China's Territorial Disputes (Princeton Studies
in International History and Politics).* Princeton University
Press, 2008, 19.

76. Saksena, Abhishek, 'The Hero of Nathula Pass – Ghost
Of Baba Harbhajan Singh That Guards India's Border,'
India Today, 23 November 2015, https://www.indiatimes.
com/culture/who-we-are/the-hero-%20of-nathula-pass-
ghost-of-baba-harbhajan-singh-that-%20guards-India-s-
border-247635.html

77. Unnithan, Sandeep, '38 Years after Death, Capt Harbhajan
Singh Guards Border with China "in Spirit",' *India Today,* 31
January 2012, https://www.indiatoday.in/magazine/offtrack/

story/20061016-capt-harbhajan-singh-guards-indo-china-border-after-death-784503-2006-10-16
78. The two sides haven't fought despite repeated provocations and stand-offs. There has been one stray incident of firing since then. On 20 October 1975, at Tulung La near Mago, four Assam Rifles soldiers were killed by Chinese firing. These were the last lives lost on either side of the LAC.

Appendix 1

Hierarchy of military units and formations in the battles of Cho La and Nathu La

Command	Eastern Command, based in Kolkata, commanded by Lieutenant General Sam Manekshaw.
Corps	33 Corps based in Siliguri, commanded by Lieutenant General Jagjit Singh Aurora.
Division	17 Division based in Gangtok, commanded by Major General Sagat Singh.
Brigade	112 Brigade based in Chhanggu, Sikkim, commanded by Brigadier M.M.S. Bakshi.
Battalion	2nd Grenadiers commanded by Lieutenant Colonel Rai Singh, 7/11 Gorkha Rifles commanded by Lieutenant Colonel K.B. Joshi, 10 Jak Rifles and 18 Rajput Regiment.
	Supporting units of Artillery, Signals and Engineers.
Company	Infantry companies were at border outposts (BOPs) and fought the battles at Nathu La and then at Cho La.
	Companies were commanded by, among others, Major Bishan Singh and Lieutenant Ram Singh Rathore.
Platoon	These subunits are part of the company.
Section	

Appendix 2

Dramatis Personae

Duane Ramsdell Clarridge

Duane 'Dewey' Clarridge was an American officer of the CIA officer. In 1965 he went to Jeddah to meet an Indian politician who had promised to share important details about an upcoming attack on India. Clarridge was later the chief of the Latin American division of the CIA from 1981 to 1987. He passed away in 2016.

Major General Sagat Singh

Sagat Singh led the military operation against the Portuguese to liberate Goa in 1961. He led 17 Division in Sikkim that fought the Nathu La and Cho La battles in 1967. As lieutenant general, he went on to lead a corps in the capture of Dhaka in 1971. Sagat is arguably India's greatest battlefield general. Intriguingly, he retired without any decoration or gallantry award. Sagat passed away in 2003.

Appendix 2: Dramatis Personae

Hope Cooke

Hope Cooke was an American national who married Palden Thondup, the Chogyal of Sikkim, and became the Gyalmo or queen at Palden Thondup Chogyal's coronation in 1965. Her advocacy for Sikkim's autonomy resulted in the souring of ties between the monarchy and the central government in Delhi. She later separated from the Chogyal and returned to the US.

Palden Thondup

Palden Thondup Namgyal was the twelfth and last Chogyal of the kingdom of Sikkim. He was also an honorary colonel of the 8th Gorkha Rifles Regiment. He was deposed through a palace takeover by the Indian government in 1975.

Lieutenant Colonel K.B. Joshi

Kul Bhushan Joshi led 7/11 Gorkha Rifles in the Cho La battle of 1967. He retired after his military service and settled in Dehradun where he lives with his two dogs.

Lieutenant Colonel Rai Singh

Rai Singh was the commanding officer of the 2nd Grenadiers battalion in Nathu La. He got injured in the battle and had to be airlifted from the scene. One of the bullets is said to have been lodged in his body forever. He retired from military service in the rank of brigadier and settled in Delhi, where he passed away in 2017.

Major Bishan Singh

Bishan was a 2nd Grenadiers company commander at Nathu La and was present when the battle broke out. He was injured in the initial stages but continued to fight as well as exhort his soldiers. He retired as a colonel and settled in Jaipur, Rajasthan.

Rifleman Debi Prasad Limbu

Young Debi of the 7/11 Gorkha Rifles died in action at Cho La and was awarded a Vir Chakra for his outstanding bravery. Debi's parents came to Delhi from Nepal to collect the award.

Havildar Tinjong Lama

Tinjong of the 7/11 Gorkha Rifles surprised the Chinese with his RCL in Cho La and swung the course of the battle by destroying Chinese bunkers. Tinjong retired in the rank of an honorary captain and settled in the hills of his native Lamahatta near Darjeeling.

Lieutenant Ram Singh Rathore

Ram Singh Rathore of the 7/11 Gorkha Rifles hailed from Rajasthan and was fond of rifle shooting. He fought valiantly in Cho La and died in action, battling the Chinese while leading his troops.

Lieutenant P.S. Dagar
Dagar of the 2nd Grenadiers died in action at Nathu La, while charging at the Chinese posts. His family lives in the NCR region and is still deeply connected with the 2nd Grenadiers battalion.

Major Harbhajan Singh
Harbhajan was from the Rajput regiment, but his platoon was brought in from the nearby pass of Yak La and deployed at Nathu La to reinforce the 2nd Grenadiers. Harbhajan died in action at Nathu La.

Captain Narayan Parulekar
Narayan was the adjutant of the 7/11 Gorkha Rifles battalion during the Cho La battle in 1967. He assisted K.B. Joshi as they launched a counterattack against the Chinese to regain the post. Narayan left the army early to become a banker in Hong Kong and later settled in Pune after retirement.

Lieutenant General Sam Manekshaw
Sam Manekshaw was the General Officer Commanding of Eastern Command (GOC in C) in 1967 and then the

hero of the 1971 war as the army chief. Interestingly, the senior command during Nathu La and Cho La replicated itself in the 1971 war, with Sam Manekshaw, Jagjit Aurora and Sagat Singh leading India against Pakistan (among other senior commanders).

Sam was the first field marshal of the Indian army and retired from active service in 1973.

V. Raghunath

Raghunath joined the Indian foreign service in 1962. In 1967 Chinese authorities expelled Raghunath and another Indian diplomat on charges of espionage. India retaliated by expelling two members of the Chinese embassy in New Delhi. Raghunath became India's foreign secretary on 1 July 1997 when he took over from Salman Haidar. On his appointment, the Chinese vice minister of foreign affairs, Tang Jiaxuan remarked, 'We welcome this appointment and congratulate him.'

Y.B. Chavan

Chavan was the defence minister of India during the 1965 war and was instrumental in improving the relationship between the armed forces and the government, after the shaky relationship between the two in the 1962 war, to one of mutual trust.

Lal Bahadur Shastri

Shastri became the prime minister of India after Jawaharlal Nehru passed away in 1964. He led India in the war against Pakistan in 1965 but passed away in Tashkent after the war. Shastri coined the term 'Jai Jawan Jai Kisan' – translated as 'Hail the soldier and the farmer', which became a nationwide slogan during those years.

Ayub Khan

Ayub Khan was the president of Pakistan during the 1965 war against India. His popularity started to go down after a mixed response to the war in his country. During his tenure, Pakistan swung from trying to woo India to becoming China's all-weather friend.

Indira Gandhi

Indira Gandhi was India's prime minister for most part of the 1960s, 1970s and early 1980s. During her tenure, India won the battles against China in 1967 and the war against Pakistan in 1971. She was assassinated in 1984.

Atal Bihari Vajpayee

Atal led a flock of sheep protestors to the Chinese embassy in 1965. In 2003, as India's prime minister, he opened the Nathu La pass for trade once again. Atal Bihari Vajpayee passed away in 2018.

Zhou Enlai

Chinese premier who had an interesting role to play during the India–Pakistan wars of 1965 and 1971. He was the Chinese premier in 1967 too.

Appendix 3

Rank structure in the Indian army

Commissioned Officer Ranks	Notes
Field Marshal	Field marshal is the highest attainable rank in the Indian army, largely ceremonial. SHFJ (Sam) Manekshaw, who features in the 1967 battles and the 1971 war, is one of the two field marshals that India has produced until now.
General	A general is the chief of the Indian army. In 1967, General P.P. Kumaramangalam was the army chief. Sam Manekshaw was the army chief during the 1971 war.
Lieutenant General	A lieutenant general can lead a command (currently, there are 7 commands in the Indian army) or a corps or can be appointed in various other staff and operational roles. 33 Corps, based in Siliguri oversaw the jurisdiction that included Sikkim. Lieutenant General Sagat Singh was the corps commander and led the Indian army's attack on Dhaka in the 1971 war.

Major General	Major general heads a division of the army. Sagat, as a major general and commander of 17 Division, led the battles against China in 1967. He was later promoted to lieutenant general before the 1971 war.
Brigadier	Brigades are commanded by brigadiers. 112 Infantry Brigade oversaw the battle at Nathu La, with Brigadier M.M.S. Bakshi at the helm.
Colonel	Colonels command the battalions, among holding other mid-level appointments in the Indian army. Rai Singh and K.B. Joshi led their troops as battalion commanders in Nathu La and Cho La respectively.
Lieutenant Colonel	Most officers who fought at Nathu La and Cho La were from these ranks.
Major	
Captain	
Lieutenant	
Second Lieutenant (the rank has now been abolished)	

Rank structure of JCOs, NCOs and riflemen

Subedar Major	They are also called junior commissioned officers or JCOs.
Subedar	
Naib Subedar	
Havildar	Called non-commissioned officers (NCOs) and other ranks. Many of the soldiers who fought at Nathu La and Cho La were NCOs and other ranks, including Tinjong Lama and Debi Prasad Limbu.
Naik	
Lance Naik	
Rifleman or Sepoy	

Appendix 4

Timeline

October–November 1962: India and China engage in a border war. China gains territories and India suffers large-scale losses.

8 April 1964: Sheikh Abdullah, the prominent political leader in Kashmir is released from prison after charges of conspiring against the state are withdrawn against him.

February 1965: Zhou Enlai meets Sheikh Abdullah in Algiers and shares an important piece of information with him.

February 1965: A strategic war game or crisis game is being played out in Arlington at a think tank supported by the US government. The crisis game envisages a war between India and Pakistan, involving China.

March 1965: Duane Clarridge, the CIA spy meets Sheikh Abdullah in Jeddah and reveals key information about the war.

August 1965: Operation Gibraltar launched by Pakistan against India in Kashmir using guerrillas and irregulars to fight covertly.

September 1965: Operation Grand Slam launched by Pakistan against India. Breakout of full-scale war on India's western front. Pakistan makes initial territorial gains but India counterattacks and takes the war into Pakistan.

China raises issues against India, alleging building of bunkers by India inside Chinese territory.

China moves troops to Nathu La and Jelep La and adopts an aggressive posture. Tensions at the two passes, Nathu La and Jelep La. Arguments continue between India and China over border violations. China issues multiple ultimatums and threatens India to end the war with Pakistan.

United Nations Security Council votes for India and Pakistan to accept a cease fire and revert to prewar positions. India–Pakistan war ends on 22 September in a stalemate with India gaining the edge over Pakistan. China continues to pressurise India at Nathu La and Jelep La at the Sikkim–Tibet border.

10 January 1966: Peace treaty is signed between India and Pakistan in the city of Tashkent. China continues to back Pakistan. Indian Prime Minister Lal Bahadur Shastri dies of a heart attack in Tashkent.

1966: After Shastri's death, the Congress legislative party elects Indira Gandhi over Morarji Desai as their leader. Indira Gandhi takes over briefly as prime minister, before the elections of 1967.

October 1966: China moves troops into Doklam plateau at the Bhutan–China border. India protests vehemently. Troops are removed soon afterwards.

14–21 February 1967: General elections take place in India. Congress Party is elected via a reduced verdict but loses absolute majority for the first time in national elections after the country's independence. There is widespread disenchantment over rising prices of commodities and unemployment.

May 1967: Internal security issues torment a newly elected prime minister. Violence erupts in Naxalbari in West Bengal. A local extremist communist movement takes shape, gets China's support and is covered in the newspapers in Peking.

13–24 June 1967: Spying scandal engulfs two Indian diplomats in Peking. Two Indian diplomats arrested and deported to India on 13 June 1965. India responds against Chinese diplomats in Delhi, detains them and then expels them from India. The two countries lurch close to a conflict.

1967: Relations further strain between the two countries as reports come in of attacks on local Indians living in China. Reports of desecration of a Sikh gurudwara in Tientsin (now Tianjin) and a Parsi temple in Shanghai add to the tension.

11–14 September 1967: Arguments erupt between Indian and Chinese troops at Nathu La leading to a battle. India avenges its defeat of the 1962 war and gives China a bloody nose.

1 October 1967: Fifteen days after the battle of Nathu La, arguments at the border at Cho La lead to another clash between Indian and Chinese troops. China suffers another defeat at the hands of India.

1968: China's Cultural Revolution affects its relations with other countries. Foreign embassies and consulates in China are targeted. China raises the question of Nathu La once again.

1969: India moves additional troops to Bhutan as part of its training team. The Indian team would stay on permanently in Bhutan, creating a military training team that continues to be stationed in Bhutan today.

1969: Mizo separatism is successfully tackled. Lieutenant General Sagat Singh leads counter insurgency operations against Mizo separatists.

1969: Chinese attack Soviet soldiers at Zhenbao Island leading to a battle with Russian soldiers. China suffers heavy defeat.

1970: Elections are held in Bangladesh. Sheikh Mujibur Rahman wins the elections. However, Pakistani President Yahya Khan denies him the premiership. Instead, a freedom movement against Pakistan breaks out in Bangladesh.

July 1971: Kissinger pays a secret visit to China. Feigning stomache in Islamabad, Pakistan he stops over in Peking and meets Zhou Enlai, the Chinese premier.

1971: Large scale Human rights violations take place. Indira Gandhi decides to attack Pakistani forces. War breaks out on the western from and the eastern front.

December 1971: Kissinger and Nixon plead with China to pressurise India. China chooses not to threaten India at the Sikkim border, despite US pleas.

December 1971: War ends in Bangladesh. India wins the war and forces Pakistani armed forces to surrender. China unable to come to Pakistan's support.

April 1975: India takes over Sikkim by sending troops to Gangtok and taking over the palace of Chogyal Palden Thondup.

1986: Stand-off takes place between India and China at Sumdorong Chu. India emerges as the dominant side in the proceedings.

2003: Trade route opens up at Nathu La. Business begins to be transacted through the pass again, after many years.

2013–17: Decade of stand-offs. Confrontations at Depsang and Chumar take place between the two countries in 2013 and 2014. In 2017, a major stand-off happens in Doklam, reviving memories of the 1966 stand-off at the same place. Unlike 1966–67, when the battles followed, the stand-off of 2017 is resolved peacefully, despite negative media publicity.

Acknowledgements

It was during my growing up years that I first heard of the Nathu La and Cho La battles from my father, an army veteran of the India–Pakistan 1965 war, who also lived in northeast India and Sikkim. This book is a tribute to him. It is also an homage to those brave souls who laid down their lives while defending the country in the twin battles of 1967.

The journey of writing the book began in 2017. I was recounting the story of India's victory over China to my friend and journalist Sriram Karri and he suggested I write on the subject.

I am grateful to General Bipin Rawat, Indian army chief, for his early encouragement. The erudite Lieutenant General Rakesh Sharma's knowledge and guidance on sources helped immensely. The process took me to several places where I met sources with first-hand tales. I am indebted to the battle heroes Kul Bhushan Joshi, Bishan

Singh, Tinjong Lama, Sheru Thapliyal, Narayan Parulekar, Bala Ganapathy for narrating painstaking ground-level accounts of the battle scenes. Sagat Singh's granddaughter, Meghna, son, Ranvijay, and his former ADC, Major General Randhir Sinh, graciously shared notes and pictures about the period – I thank them all immensely. Major General (retd) V.K. Singh, who has written on the battle, shared his thoughts on the finer aspects.

Regimental history notes of 11 GR and Grenadiers, along with help from the 2nd Grenadiers – the Nathu La battalion – helped piece together lesser known anecdotes. Interviews with Lieutenant General J.B.S. Yadav, a 1971 war hero, Colonel B.K.D. Badgel and Gautam Das assisted in sketching the events of the 1960s. In Sikkim, the magnanimous Major General K.V.S. Lalotra helped me find my way and I was fortunate to have the support of Major General Raja Subramani, 17 Mountain Division, Sikkim Scouts and the dogged Nitin Shrestha.

The body of research couldn't have happened without the untiring efforts of the talented Mehr Gill and the meticulous Mangesh Sawant. Thanks to Jason Jacob, Mehr and Mangesh for reading my initial drafts and to Sriram for his sharp eye and wise feedback. The book wouldn't have been the same without the steady support of author and literary agent Kanishka Gupta and his team

Acknowledgements

at Writer's Side. Kanishka's astute feedback and prudent suggestions helped me stay on track.

Special thanks to Chiki Sarkar and her wonderful team at Juggernaut for the tremendous support. The calm passion and acumen of Parth Mehrotra was instrumental in honing and shaping the draft. I am indebted to him and editors Arushi Singh and Swarnima Narayan for taking the narrative from the stage of a preliminary copy to the book you are reading now.

I am grateful to friends and acquaintances who have been supportive during the journey of this book: Manish Kumar, Major General (retd) V.K. Pillai, Shankar Rajesh, Anand Sinha, Major General B.J. Gupta, Sudesh Dhanda, Lieutenant General Narasimhan, Sangram Nalwaya, Ambassador P. Stopdan, Abhishek Dwivedi, Brigadier Salil Seth, Lathika Swami. I thank S.S. Pundir, Vijay Shekhar Sharma for their prompt assistance and Vivek Naithani, who helped negotiate obstacles to track primary sources. Thanks to Manish Mall, with whom I often exchanged opinions about the subject. I wish to thank the other publishers who showed interest in the early stage of the book idea. I also owe a special note of gratitude to my schoolteacher, Ahmed Ansari, who taught me to write early on.

Lastly, the book would never have been complete

Acknowledgements

without the love and support of my wife, Nisha, and her unwavering belief in my work, despite my absences on account of research and work. Thanks to my children – Siddharth and Arayna – who had to patiently endure my repetitive stories, and my mother, Shyamla, who has been a steady, calm support. Grateful to my brother, Protip, who has been one of the most passionate backers of the story.

I am also obliged to the various authors of articles, books, notes, research material available on the subject that helped me complete the book. *Watershed 1967* does not seek to provide a historical account of conflicts involving India and China, as there are more detailed accounts by several historians. Instead, this book delves into a gap in the established historical narrative to identify the role of a forgotten conflict in India–China relations and its impact on the events that followed.

juggernaut

THE APP FOR INDIAN READERS

Fresh, original books tailored for mobile and for India. Starting at ₹10.

juggernaut.in

CRAFTED FOR MOBILE READING

Thought you would never read a book on mobile? Let us prove you wrong.

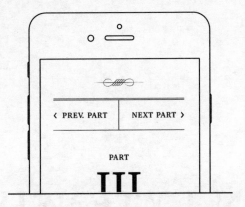

Beautiful Typography

The quality of print transferred
to your mobile. Forget ugly PDFs.

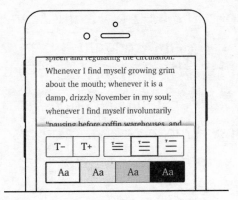

Customizable Reading

Read in the font size, spacing
and background of your liking.

AN EXTENSIVE LIBRARY

Including fresh, new, original Juggernaut books from the likes of Sunny Leone, Praveen Swami, Husain Haqqani, Umera Ahmed, Rujuta Diwekar and lots more. Plus, books from partner publishers and loads of free classics. Whichever genre you like, there's a book waiting for you.

DON'T JUST READ; INTERACT

We're changing the reading experience from passive to active.

Ask authors questions

Get all your answers from the horse's mouth.
Juggernaut authors actually reply to every
question they can.

Rate and review

Let everyone know of your favourite reads or
critique the finer points of a book – you will be
heard in a community of like-minded readers.

Gift books to friends

For a book-lover, there's no nicer gift than
a book personally picked. You can even
do it anonymously if you like.

Enjoy new book formats

Discover serials released in parts over
time, picture books including comics,
and story-bundles at discounted rates.
And coming soon, audiobooks.

LOWEST PRICES & ONE-TAP BUYING

Books start at ₹10 with regular discounts and free previews.

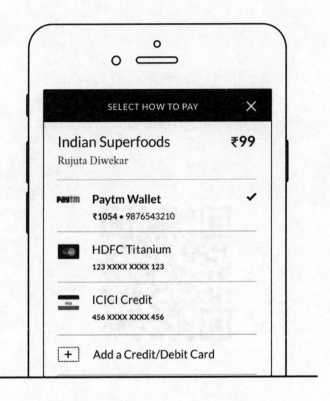

Paytm Wallet, Cards & Apple Payments

On Android, just add a Paytm Wallet once and buy any book with one tap. On iOS, pay with one tap with your iTunes-linked debit/credit card.

Click the QR Code with a QR scanner app
or type the link into the Internet browser
on your phone to download the app.

For our complete catalogue, visit www.juggernaut.in
To submit your book, send a synopsis and two
sample chapters to books@juggernaut.in
For all other queries, write to contact@juggernaut.in